24 95

Don Gresswell Ltd., London, N21   Cat. No. 1207   DG 02242/71

Developing managerial competences

Developing managerial competences

The Management Learning Contract approach

George Boak

with David Thompson and Lindsay Mitchell

Foreword by Mike Day

Pitman

Pitman Publishing
128 Long Acre, London WC2E 9AN

A Division of Longman Group UK Limited

First published in 1991

British Library Cataloguing in Publication Data
Boak, George
    Developing managerial competences.
    1. Management
    I. Title II. Thompson, David III. Mitchell, Lindsay
    658

ISBN 0-273-03326-3

Printed in Great Britain by The Bath Press, Avon

Contents

Mike Day
Executive director of the Management Charter Initiative, formerly with IBM

Lindsay Mitchell
Director of research and development at Barbara Shelborn Developments Ltd

David Thompson
Senior consultant with Northern Regional Management Centre

George Boak
Programme manager with Northern Regional Management Centre

Foreword

When the small team at the centre of the Management Charter Initiative started looking around for exemplars of good practice in management training and development, it was suggested we look at the Northern Regional Management Centre. We visited the Centre at Washington, Tyne and Wear, and were impressed with what we saw, particularly with the enthusiasm shown by the local employers for the activities of the Centre. What we found was a highly developed form of action learning, apparently meeting the needs of both individuals and employers. At the heart of this we met John Gritton, Mac Stephenson and George Boak, and I am glad to say that the association has continued. George, in particular, has played a valued part in the development of Management Competence Standards for the MCI and the Training Agency.

From all the findings of the Handy and Constable, and other reports, one must conclude that most managers in the UK get most of their development through on-the-job experience. The main work of NRMC is in the exploitation of this process through Management Learning Contracts, the subject of the book. One of its great virtues is that the process harnesses the efforts of the individual, his manager and an outside educator or trainer so that all three parties benefit both directly and indirectly. When coupled with effective methods for needs analysis such as the competence standards, the results are development activities and management qualifications which really can benefit everyone involved.

As with all worthwhile activities and processes, there is much to be learned from the early pioneers in the field and that is why this book should be of great value to trainers, developers, educators and to managers themselves. The case studies which describe in detail how to identify tasks which combine learning opportunities for the individual with direct benefits to the organisation, should open the eyes of employers to the potential benefits of this approach. These same potential benefits should help managers to gain support for their education and development from the organisation. The detail on the guidance on how to use this process should help all concerned who want to implement the learning contract methodology. For those in education, the book also provides an insight into how this methodology relates to qualifications in the management area. One of the most impressive things about NRMC is the way they have put together a complete progressive training and development programme, providing appropriate qualification programmes from supervisor to senior manager: all these qualifications are heavily dependent on learning contracts.

By helping all concerned to implement more effective and less costly development programmes based on the learning contract approach, this book will be making a significant contribution to the quality of management and supervision in the UK.

Mike Day
Management Charter Initiative

Introduction

The Management Learning Contract is a method of helping people to learn skills, acquire knowledge and develop whatever competences they want or need in relation to their work. When it is used correctly, the MLC method is probably the best way to motivate managers to learn and to support them while they are developing.

The purpose of this book is to encourage and to help those involved in training and development to use the Management Learning Contract method effectively, without making more than the inevitable number of initial mistakes. It assumes no previous knowledge, so it will suit the complete beginner. It goes into the details of how to deal with difficult situations, so it will also, I hope, have something useful to say to the more seasoned practitioner. It has been written on the basis of experience in using MLCs with a large number of managers over the past five years, and it aims to provide a practical guide to the opportunities and problems.

The competence movement of recent years, the numerous attempts to define the skills and the behaviours of effective managers, have achieved on a comprehensive scale what we have been doing only piecemeal with the learning objectives of individual MLCs. The models of competence have created a framework within which managers can plot their development, and plan their individual course. The MLC method can help them to define and to reach their goals.

Throughout the book there are short case studies, anecdotes and examples of the efforts of individual learners and managers. (The names have been changed to protect us all from embarrassment.) Without their efforts, aims, desires, eagerness and obstinacy this book could not have been written. Nor could it have been completed without the aid of the staff of the Northern Regional Management Centre, whose contributions have ranged from the vision of the design of the MLC method to critical analysis of its implementation, from ruthless debate about first principles to unhesitating support.

George Boak 1990

Part One

Competences

Management competences have been defined in two ways.

The predominant approach in the United States, and in some UK companies, has been to identify and define key skills, qualities and behaviours associated with effective managers.

More recently the methods used to establish occupational standards for other jobs have been applied to the management role. The approach here is to define the required behaviour in terms of its results.

The two chapters which follow explain the two complementary approaches.

Chapter 1

Competences: qualities and skills

When you have completed this chapter you should be able to:

- **explain the relationship between competences and effective management.**
- **recognise and give examples of competence definitions.**
- **set out the advantages, uses and difficulties of generic competence models.**
- **describe how competences can be assessed and developed.**

Introduction

One approach to improving the effectiveness of a company's management is to learn what qualities and skills are possessed by effective managers and then, through selection, training and development, put effective individuals in all key posts.

This, in essence, is the approach of the competence movement.

- A competent manager is an effective manager.
- Competences are the relevant qualities and skills that lead to effective job performance.

In the last ten years, research in this area has generated a great many typologies of qualities and skills and behaviours associated with effective managers in particular jobs.

In seeking to define the personal qualities or characteristics of the effective manager, the competence movement appears at first sight to be covering ground once well trodden and now abandoned. One of the earliest assumptions about people who lead and manage others was that their effectiveness was due to inherent personal qualities – Vision, Vitality, Decisiveness, Persuasiveness and so on. This gave rise to various 'Great Man' theories, still common in the 1940s and 1950s, before they gave way to the simple functional approach (see Box 1.1).

The simple functional approach focussed on what managers are expected to do: the Planning, Organising, Motivating and Controlling and so on. More effective management would come about by training managers in each of these functions. Of course, this was old ground, too, already well covered by early writers on management. But the new systems perspectives cast Organising and Controlling in a different light, the corporate vision and decision theory enlivened.

Box 1.1 The Great Man

'Perhaps because of historical antecedents from Machiavelli back to Plato, the first focus of thought on managerial effectiveness was to look at the manager himself – the person – and to assume that effectiveness resulted from inherent qualities within the manager, or leader . . .

'A picture emerged of effective management as being "a mixture of Samuel Smiles and Field Marshal Montgomery" . . . and of the effective manager as being a "universal genius" . . . Qualities such as high intelligence, assertiveness, extraversion, decisiveness, ambition and emotional stability were felt to be essential for effective managers. It is perhaps a truism to say that those who have these qualities may still not be effective managers and that those who do not may still be effective.' (*Langford 1979*)

A good example of the genre is Chester Barnard, who picked out five fundamental qualities or characteristics of those who are leaders as: 'Vitality and Endurance, Decisiveness, Persuasiveness, Responsibility, and Intellectual Capacity.' (*Barnard 1948*)

Planning, the more humanitarian ideas of employee relations brought a fresh appearance to Motivation, and generally there was more to learn for the manager who wanted to be more effective.

Box 1.2 Everything is possible

Perhaps the spirit of the return to an assessment of management functions is seen most clearly in the area of Motivation Theory. Douglas McGregor's Theory Y which encouraged managers to see those who worked for them as willing and able individuals, for whom 'work was as natural as rest or play', emphasised the trust in the capability of people to learn and develop that is an implicit hallmark of the simple functional approach. (*McGregor 1961*)

At the same time David McClelland was developing and writing about an approach to motivation that aimed to assess the habitual drives and behaviour patterns of individuals: a very different approach to that of McGregor, or of Maslow and Hertzberg, and one which was to grow into the competence movement (see Box 1.14).

In severe contrast to McGregor's optimism is the advice of an early writer on management and administration: 'In the first place' the administrator can hardly ever make too much allowance for the indolence of mankind. Where his administration will fail, is in people omitting to do, from indolence, that which he supposes he has given them sufficient means and instructions for doing. Hence, in all matters of administration, continuous supervision and inspection are most needful, as is also great preciseness of instruction.

Box 1.2 continued

In the next place, he must calculate upon a large amount of disobedience, resulting, not from wilfulness, but from misunderstanding, or from the subordinate "thinking", as he is pleased to call it, for himself, when he has received precise directions from his superior.' (*Helps 1872*)

The rise of the competence movement in the past ten years is an indication that the simple functional approach is insufficient.

The interest in the qualities and skills of the effective manager had never completely vanished. At the very least, it was kept alive by recruitment specialists and the purveyors of psychometric tests. The competence movement returned this area of interest to the management development agenda. The various models of competent managers that have been produced in this period represent an advance on the pre-war Great Man theories in so far as they:

- relate competences to observable actions and behaviours, so they can be tested.
- are based on, or tested in, practice.
- take into account the contingencies of the job to be done.

Defining competences

A rigorous procedure for defining competences has emerged from the specialists in the field.

- First, define effectiveness: decide what counts as effective performance of a specific managerial job. This will involve discussions, at an appropriate level in the organisation, about the output and behaviour required of particular managerial posts.
- Second, select samples: identify a sample of managers who are considered to be effective and a sample of managers who are considered to be below standard. This is done by various means of senior manager and peer assessment. The actual groups chosen may be 'highly effective', 'average', 'poor'.
- Third, identify the competences: using a variety of tests and interviews, the skills and qualities of the sample groups are assessed. In particular, the characteristics that distinguish the effective from the ineffective managers are sought. Further tests with another sample may then be carried out to validate the findings (see Box 1.3).

Box 1.3 The experts

'In one study, interviews had been conducted with eighteen supposedly outstanding employee relations managers; upon reading the transcripts, however, we had to report to the client organisation that three of these people did not seem to be outstanding, at which point the client reported that these three average performers had been included in the outstanding sample to test us.' (*Klemp 1986*)

The front runners of the competence movement were the staff of McBer and Company and of Charles River Consulting, Boston, Massachusetts.

This is no more than a sensible, systematic procedure, of course: we identify the results we want (high output, good staff morale, detailed plans for the future, etc.); then we identify which managers provide those results; then we take a close look at them to see what makes them different from the rest.

This procedure produces a range of behaviours, skills and attitudes. We may find, for example, that our effective managers are more likely to:

- act patiently and calmly in situations of continuing high pressure.
- take explicit action to reduce the effects of personal stress without noticeable deterioration of their performance.
- maintain high performance and attention to detail while working on a prolonged task. (*AMA 1982*)

Box 1.4 Competencies, competences and behavioural indicators

George Klemp has defined a competency as 'an underlying characteristic of a person which results in effective and/or superior performance in a job'.

(Klemp 1980)

This focusses attention on the quality that enables or gives rise to skilled behaviour.

The large-scale study by McBer and Company (Box 1.7), aimed to explore not only skills, but also Traits, Motives, Self Images and Social Roles. The bulk of the conclusive evidence, however, was gathered at the level of skill, very close to the indicating (or defining) behaviours. Traits were only significant in two competence areas; motives likewise in two areas; social role – the expectations of others – in nine areas; skill in fifteen out of the total of eighteen areas.

(Boyatzis 1982)

The Americans and, following them, some British writers, have used the words 'competency' and 'competencies' more loosely than Klemp to refer to the qualities and skills of competent managers. On the whole, throughout this book the word *competence* has been used, to mean the same thing.

The first list is unlikely to be brief. A list of the skills and behaviours of effective School Principals by McBer and Company, for example, is 45 items long. An analysis of the competences of senior managers by Charles River Consulting identified 21 separate items. (*Klemp 1986*)

For obvious operational reasons, the items are organised into logical clusters, and in many cases it is at this stage that a group of behaviours or skills is given a label that implies a quality or characteristic. These groups are referred to as the Competences, and the original behaviours and skills as the Behavioural Indicators – the means by which we may recognise the competences.

So, for example, the three skills we may expect from our effective managers (above) are all indicators of the competence of Stamina and Adaptability. (*AMA 1982*)

The typical shape of a competence model of this type, therefore, is of a number of characteristics – which may be expressed as qualities, for example, Self Confidence, Proactivity, Self Control – each accompanied by a number of Behavioural Indicators, which define the competence in action.

Not all competence models are the results of this particular rigorous and systematic research process. Some company models appear to have their origins in what managers *think* are necessary skills for effective performance (*Greatrex and Phillips 1989; Glaze 1989; Green 1987*), and these original suppositions are then modified in the light

---

Box 1.5 Seeing is believing

The relationship between competences and observable behaviours is crucial. It separates the modern competence movement from the vague Great Man theories. In many respects the Behavioural Indicators are more important than the competences that form the group title for the family.

Some in-company examples bear out this point. For example, under the competence heading of 'Team Management', British Petroleum provide a scale of five behaviours, sketched in brief pen-portraits, with a further list of seven indicators of behaviours for each end of the scale. (*Greatrex and Phillips 1989*)

A recent report notes 'The use of behaviourally anchored rating scales is also becoming more popular. In this approach each aspect of skill language is described in terms of expected behaviour and the rating scale has for each level a behavioural description of that level of performance. This does not necessarily exclude the use of vague terms such as "leadership" as criteria but does go a long way towards clarifying what the organisation expects a "good leader" to look like doing their job. Behavioural descriptions of skill have the added virtue that assessing behaviour in particular task areas is probably how managers naturally assess each other anyway.' (*Hirsh and Bevan 1988*)

of experience. To summarise: if effective performance of a job is the achievement of specific results by approved means, and the individual's competences are the skills that enable him/her to be effective, then by defining the competences required for a particular job we can:

- recruit and select, using the competences as criteria.
- analyse skill needs and help individuals to develop in appropriate ways.
- discuss, agree and carry out joint policies of selection and development, using the shared language of our competences model (see Box 1.6).

Box 1.6 Competences in context

Where the demands of the job are congruent with the culture and environment of the organisation and with the competences of the individual, there will be sustained, effective performance of the job.

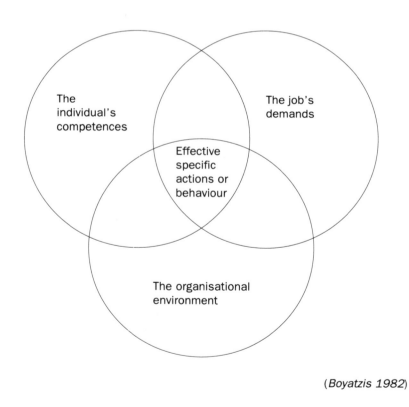

(*Boyatzis 1982*)

Box 1.6 continued

This admits the possibility of an individual whose skills do not match the demands of a particular job and the possibility of an individual whose skills and qualities lead to a maverick approach to a job, outside the rules and procedures expected by the organisation.

The competence standards approach (see Chapter 2) focusses more explicitly on the demands of the job.

We will return to both assessment and development later in this chapter, but before doing that we should explore the next step taken by the competence movement: the generic models.

Generic competences

The competence movement quickly went beyond the analysis and definition of competences for a particular job, to produce a number of models of manager competence that claim to be generic: in other words, they set out qualities and skills of effective managers across a range of organisations.

The advantages of a generic model – if accurate – are obvious:

- Individuals with the full range of generic competences would be able to manage in a wide variety of situations.
- The competences in the model could serve as the basis for all management development.
- The expense of thoroughly analysing the competences required for effective performance of any particular job can be avoided.

The difficulty of accepting the accuracy of such a model is also obvious. It ignores the specific demands of the particular job. Even if we accept the notion of generic competences, the demands of a particular job are likely to weight the desirability of certain parts of the model, making some competences crucial to effective performance and others relatively unimportant.

The American Management Association commissioned McBer and Company, a behavioural research firm from Boston, to research and define a model of generic management competences in the late 1970s. The research was extensive (see Box 1.7).

The results were 65 behaviours, skills and attitudes, organised into 18 groups. Six of the groups were defined as *threshold competences* in that they were seen as essential to adequate job performance. Twelve

---

Box 1.7 McBer research: an initial attempt

The McBer research covered over 1000 managers, in eight private sector and four public sector organisations.

The majority of positive findings from the research – the identification of skills associated with superior managers – come from the Behavioural Event Interviews carried out with 253 managers, from ten different organisations (eight private, two public sector). The average length of the interview was two hours.

Only two coders were used to analyse the transcripts. They were coding without an awareness of whether the manager was supposedly 'superior', 'average' or 'poor'. Regular checks were carried out to ensure consistency.

Distinctions were made between levels of management, described here as 'entry', 'middle' and 'executive'.

The Chief Executive Officer of McBer and Company notes: 'A word of caution is in order regarding the summary and potential application of the findings from this study. First, the study was an initial attempt to determine what a generic competency model of management should include . . . '

(Boyatzis 1982 p. 231)

---

of the groups were competences possessed more often by superior managers than by average or poor managers.

Box 1.8 American Management Association

The eighteen groups uncovered by McBer and Company were divided into actual competencies (the possession of which distinguishes the superior from the average manager) and *threshold competencies* (which appeared to be essential to doing the job).

The competency groups were:

Efficiency Orientation – Concern with doing something better.
Proactivity – Disposition toward initiating activity.
Concern with Impact – Concern with the symbols and uses of power.
Diagnostic Use of Concepts – Use of previously held concepts to explain and interpret situations
Use of Unilateral Power – Use of forms of influence
Developing Others – Ability to provide performance feedback.
Spontaneity – Ability to express oneself freely and easily.
Accurate Self-Assessment – Realistic and grounded view of oneself.
Self-Control – Ability to inhibit personal needs.
Stamina and Adaptability – The energy to sustain long hours of work and the flexibility to adapt to changes.
Perceptual Objectivity – Ability to be relatively objective.
Positive Regard – Ability to express a positive belief in others.

Box 1.8 continued

Managing Group Process – Ability to stimulate others to work effectively in a group setting.

Use of Socialised Power – Use of influence to build alliances, networks, or coalitions.

Self-Confidence – Ability consistently to display decisiveness or presence.

Conceptualisation – Use of new concepts to identify a pattern in an assortment of information.

Logical Thought – Order events in a causal sequence.

Use of Oral Presentations – Ability to make effective oral presentations to others.

Accurate Self Assessment, Positive Regard, Developing Others, Spontaneity, Use of Unilateral Power and Logical Thought were threshold competencies.

Managing Group Processes and Conceptualisation appeared to be competencies at middle and senior levels of management only.

The possession and mastery of Specialised Knowledge relevant to the job was seen as an important attribute (although there was no evidence that Memory was a competency) such that Specialised Knowledge is described as a nineteenth (threshold) competency. (*Boyatzis 1982*)

In a later project, Klemp and McClelland analysed the results of six separate pieces of competence research in different organisational

Box 1.9 Klemp and McClelland and Schroder

The Klemp and McClelland model is based on six other studies. In all, 132 managers were interviewed, fifty-six of whom were considered 'outstanding' and the remainder 'average'.

The competence groups were:

Planning/causal thinking	Directive influence
Diagnostic information seeking	Collaborative influence
Conceptualisation/synthetic thinking	Symbolic influence
Concern for influence	Self-confidence

(*Klemp 1986*)

The competence model developed by Harry Schroder in Florida has eleven competence groupings. These are:

Information search	Achievement orientation
Concept formation	Interpersonal search
Conceptual flexibility	Managing interaction
Presentation skills	Development orientation
Self-confidence	Impact
Proactive orientation	

(*Cockerill 1989*)

sectors to derive the generic competences of outstanding senior managers. The result is a list of 21 skills and behaviours, organised into eight groups (see Box 1.9). Although the behaviours are sometimes grouped differently, there are striking similarities between this and the AMA model.

In the UK, Government-funded research through the Training Agency and the National Forum for Management Education and Development (NFMED) investigated management competences from 1988 to 1990. The main thrust of the project was to define competence standards in the form of outputs and productive behaviour, and to establish competence standards, as described in Chapter 2, but one part of the project considered competences as qualities and skills in the same way as the Americans.

The result is a model of 13 competences, with 80 behavioural indicators, covering similar skills and qualities to those observed in the American research.

Box 1.10 Personal effectiveness: the MCI model

The competences are gathered in four clusters. They represent personal effectiveness competences which will lead to best practice in management.

Cluster 1: Showing Concern for Excellence
Setting and Prioritising Objectives
Monitoring and Responding to Actual against Planned Activities

Cluster 2: Showing Sensitivity to the Needs of Others
Relating to Others
Obtaining the Commitment of Others
Presenting Oneself Positively to Others

Cluster 3: Showing Self-Confidence and Personal Drive
Managing Personal Emotions and Stress
Managing Personal Learning and Development

Cluster 4: Collecting and Organising Information
Identifying and Applying Concepts
Taking Decisions.

The evidence for the existence of certain generic management competences, irrespective of the specific details of the job, is reasonably strong, but not conclusive. The generic models in circulation have been derived from an analysis of practice and they are usable for assessment and development.

They offer any company the chance to:

- base recruitment and development activities for particular posts on a generic model, after a considered weighting of the desired qualities and skills in the light of the demands of the specific post and/or
- use a generic model for recruitment and development on the basis that the dynamics of change, particularly at senior levels, will require the full range of qualities and skills (see Box 1.11) and/or
- develop a company-specific model by amending the generic model to take account of the culture, priorities and common language of the company.

These are opportunities to be taken seriously.

Box 1.11 Preparing for Change

'A thorough review of the literature and of management development practices across the world revealed that very little work had been undertaken to prepare managers for more dynamic environments. However, one initiative did seem to be far ahead of anything else: that led by Harry Schroder, former Professor of Psychology at Princeton and now Professor of Management at the University of South Florida. He had drawn on several areas of research to identify and test the validity of 11 "High performance managerial competencies" . . . and subsequent research in NatWest to test his findings strongly indicates that high levels of performance are achieved in changing circumstances when managers use the competencies.' (*Cockerill 1989*)

The IMS report notes that

- more employers are using internal research to establish descriptions of the qualities and skills they seek.
- for effective assessment of individuals for the required qualities and skills, descriptions of desirable features of behaviour which the assessor can observe are a useful and practical approach.
- more should be done to define and assess for the skills likely to be needed by managers in the future.

(*Hirsh and Bevan 1988*)

Assessing competences

Efforts have been made to assess the qualities and skills of individual managers:

- when researching a competence model, as part of the process of taking a close look at effective managers to see what distinguishes them from the pack.

- at the start of a programme of individual development, to establish the learning needs of participants.

Three types of approach have been taken: the Behavioural Event Interview, Pen and Paper Tests, and Assessment Centres.

Behavioural event interviews

In the research context, as George Klemp observes, once the effective performers have been identified we might wish to follow and observe them at work and determine over a period of weeks how their behaviour differed from that of average managers: but this process would have its limitations. It would be too expensive to use with a suitable sample of managers, and it would not penetrate the thoughts and motivations of the individual. (*Klemp 1986*).

As an alternative, Klemp commends an interview method, Behavioural Event Interviewing (BEI) which is based upon the Critical Incident Interviewing (CII). (*Flanagan 1954*)

The aim of the BEI interview is to get the participating managers to describe in detail an event in which they played a part, and obtain an account of what they did, and what they thought and felt.

In doing this, the focus is on:

- specific events – not what 'often', 'normally' or 'sometimes' happens.
- the actions of the interviewee – not what other people did, or what 'we' did, but on the contributions of the individual.
- actual thoughts and deeds – not what 'on reflection' the person 'should have done'.

The aim of the interviewer is to avoid leading the participating manager, except to ensure that the discussion covers the area of actions, thoughts and feelings, and maintains the focus on specific behaviours – not behaviours or hopes for the future or retrospective evaluations.

The interview should re-construct an event (or in fact, a number of events) giving the manager an opportunity to describe competent behaviour exhibited in the past. The account of the event is then analysed to see what behaviours and possible competences it contains. (For research purposes, the interview is recorded and an analysis is carried out on the transcript. For recruitment, the account might be analysed by the interviewer as it unfolds.)

Box 1.12 Tell me about it

The Behavioural Event Interview will follow a different pattern, depending on whether it is being used to research a model of competence, or whether it is being used for assessment of an individual.

In the former case, the minimum of guidance or steerage should be employed. The aim is to understand what actions or skills separate the superior from the average, from the poor, manager. The typical opening script is: 'I want you to tell me about a time in the recent past when you felt particularly pleased with something you had achieved in relation to your job.'

The recency dimension is to guide the individual to an event which he or she will be able to recall in detail; the 'particularly pleased' aspect is to encourage the manager to present an event which he/she is keen to explain.

The interviewer seeks an explanation from the manager of what was done, what was said, what was thought and what was felt in relation to the event, using neutral questions which aim to avoid generalisations and rationalisations after the event.

Where the aim is to assess an individual by BEI (typically for recruitment and selection) the interviewer should have a clear idea of the competences sought for the post and will construct the interview to give the respondent a chance to display these competences.

The distinctive feature of this approach is an avoidance of hypothetical questions ('How would you cope with managing older supervisors?') or self-evaluative questions ('What are your main strengths?') in favour of inquiry into what has happened in the past ('Have you ever been challenged by an older supervisor? Tell me about it. What happened?').

If the competence is crucial to successful performance of the job more than one indication should be sought.

The shape of the actual interview will depend upon the experiences indicated by the individual's application form, and the interviewer must be thoughtful and inventive in fitting the specification of competences to the experiences of the applicant.

In recruitment and selection situations the Behavioural Event approach may not govern the whole interview, as the interviewer may inquire about hopes and ambitions and retrospective evaluations, as additional information to assist in his/her decision as well as to conform in some respects with the expectations of the applicant.

If the event is being analysed in an attempt to determine the differences between the effective managers in a company and those below standard, the analysis would focus on actual behaviour that led to an effective result in a specific case.

If the event is being analysed to assess individual abilities and development needs, the analysis would focus on relating individual behaviour to a particular competence model.

Both the interviewing and the coding of the interviews are skilled jobs. Interviewees differ greatly in their willingness and ability to recount the details of specific events, and it can be difficult to draw usable material from an individual who is prone to generalise, or to evaluate after the event, who prefers to discuss actions in terms of established procedures, or who talks and thinks in the team terms of the first person plural.

The approach of the interview is to give the individual respondent the opportunity to talk about his/her achievements, and thereby describe occasions when he/she displayed the skills which led to effective actions. The job of the interviewer is to keep the focus of the description on the skills and actions of the individual around certain points: decisions that were taken, interactions with other people.

The coding is often a matter of judgement, requiring discussion and consensus if there is more than one coder, about what scores and what does not, and how the behaviour can best be described.

The theory behind the method is that an individual who has demonstrated a skill in the past has the capacity to demonstrate that skill again in the future. The method does not necessarily probe motivation (will the individual *want* to use such skills in the future?) but focusses on skill and capacity, although recurrent signs of a particular skill may indicate typical as well as potential behaviours.

The advantages of the method are:

- it concentrates on actual behaviour – not on the ideal.
- it explores not only the action, but also the thoughts and feelings accompanying the action.

The difficulties are:

- *the behaviour may not be representative.* This presents a particular problem in situations where the individual is being assessed by means of this interview approach – for example at recruitment, or at some form of appraisal. This is related to the second difficulty:
- *interviewing and coding are skilled jobs.* It requires time to learn and to develop the necessary skills. A skilled BEI interviewer may well overcome many of the problems posed by the unrepresentative picture presented by the manager.

Pen and Paper Tests

We must note at this point another method that has been used to assess competences in this context – the Picture Story Exercise (PSE).

Although the AMA and Charles River models are largely based on the Behavioural Event Interview, the PSE has played a minor role.

Typically, the PSE presents an individual with a relatively ambiguous picture – usually of two or more people who are evidently engaged in some kind of dialogue – and asks the respondent to describe what is happening in the picture, what has led up to it, who is saying what. Based on Thematic Apperception Tests, the PSE lets the respondent project his/her interpretations onto ambiguous circumstances, and so reveal underlying drives and traits .

Box 1.13 Tell me a story

The use of the Picture Story Exercise was a feature of David McClelland's early work on motivation. He identified the Achievement motivation (nAch, or need for Achievement) as a particular drive that was stronger in some people than in others, and which led to effective behaviour in certain managerial positions. The Picture Story Exercise was a means of testing an individual for this drive.

After glancing at a picture for 10–15 seconds, the respondent was asked to compose a brief story, setting out who the people in the picture were, what was happening, what led up to the event, what would happen next. Typical high Achievement responses would describe the scene as part of a project, the dialogue as a discussion of plans or progress and the individuals in terms of their project roles.

Other motivational profiles identified by McClelland and his colleagues were the drive for Power and the drive for Affiliation. Identifying signs of these drives, and the drive for Achievement, were set out so that a PSE script could be coded and given an agreed grade.

McClelland's work on this stretches from the early 1950s through to the mid-1970s, by which time he was already writing about competences, and on this evidence he is clearly one of the founding fathers of the competence movement.

The Picture Story Exercise relies on projection of inner themes: the manager concerned with Achievement projects this concern onto the picture, the manager concerned with Power does the same, and in this respect it is a variety of Rorschach Test.

In the AMA Research the motives of the Achievement drive and the drive for Power were related to the competencies of Efficiency, Orientation and Concern with Impact respectively, and were present to a significant extent in the make-up of superior managers. (*Boyatzis 1982 pp. 195–204; McClelland 1953, 1958, 1961, 1973*)

As with the Behavioural Event Interview, the statements of the participating manager can be coded to assess the predominant motivations and habitual responses influencing his/her actions.

As a method of assessing competences, the PSE is much more limited than the Behavioural Event Interview. There is little evidence at present of a causal link between particular traits or motives (the characteristics assessed by the PSE) and more effective management. Also, responses to the PSE are much easier to distort by a respondent who knows what is being assessed than responses to BEI questions.

Other pen and paper tests have been used: David Kolb's Learning Style Inventory was used in the AMA research, for example, but there is no evidence to suggest that other tests enable competences to be assessed accurately, either for purposes of developing a competence model or for developing a more competent manager. (*Kolb 1976*).

Assessment centres

Assessment centres are a means of evaluating an individual's abilities against a set of required or desirable characteristics; their use goes back over 50 years.

They have been used to evaluate the competences of an individual against a model and also to refine a model for use in particular circumstances.

The features of assessment centres are:

- the individuals being assessed undertake a number of different activities and tests.
- some of the activities simulate key components of the relevant job (or role).
- the activities are observed and evaluated by several assessors.

Box 1.14 Testing

Shroder's model of generic competence has been tested in assessment centres in Florida, and in the NatWest Bank in the UK. (*Cockerill 1989*)

There are mixed views on the value and validity of assessment centres. They can provide an efficient means of assessing the skills and behaviour of managers in certain situations: the crucial question is whether the assessment reflects skills and behaviours *outside* the assessment centre, in a real job. There are also concerns about the accuracy of the assessment itself.

(*Smith and Blackham 1988*)

Their proponents argue that their accuracy is very high and that criticism of their value is based on observation of bad practice, or of events incorrectly called assessment centres.

(*Thornton and Byham 1982; Goodge and Griffiths 1985; Griffiths and Allen 1987*)

Typical activities may include presentations, analysis of case studies, group negotiations or discussions, team exercises, in-tray exercises, and interviews. Tests of ability and personality profile tests may also be used.

Summary

The methods used to assess competences in order to develop a model of good practice, or in order to assess an individual for recruitment or needs analysis purposes have been Behavioural Event Interviews, Assessment Centres, and some Pen and Paper Tests.

So far we have not touched upon how the development of competences – the enhancement of skills and knowledge – might be assessed. This is a crucial concern for all who are involved in management development. It is discussed in detail in Chapter 6.

Developing competences

One concern of the competence movement has been to produce a model which is of value in recruitment and selection. A further concern is to help individual managers develop the competences necessary for present and future job roles.

Development processes naturally concentrate on behaviour and skills which can be learned. As we have seen, the notion of competences as qualities comes about when behaviours and skills are clustered under a common heading to make the model more manageable, and there is little hard evidence of innate drives or rare traits of character playing an essential part in effective management.

An exemplary approach to the development process has been described by a member of the American Management Association (*Powers 1987*). The process can be set out as a series of stages:

- *Audit*: a group of learners/managers go through an assessment centre which includes simulations and individual Behavioural Event Interviews (which are recorded on tape) and a series of pen and paper exercises. The results are assessed by professional coders against the AMA model of 65 competences. The managers are also given a Competence Questionnaire, based on the model, which they distribute to colleagues at their workplace. There is a gap of a number of weeks between the audit and the next phase of the programme.
- *Recognition and Understanding*: the managers are introduced to the model, and the training staff help them to understand the

connections between the competences and effective job performance, and help them to recognise the competences in their own behaviour and the behaviour of those around them.

- *Accepting assessment:* the results of the audit are revealed to the managers and, combined with the results of the Competence Questionnaire distributed to colleagues, they enable the creation of a profile of strengths and areas for further development. Some of the pen and paper exercises help to establish suitable methods for development.
- *Action Planning:* individual managers draw up action plans to develop necessary skills under-represented in the profile, assisted by trainers. Opportunities are provided during this period – as the action plan is being drawn up – for the managers to practise the behaviours they desire to develop and to obtain feedback from fellow learners, trainers and videotape recordings. Managers are encouraged to develop specific plans, over a six month timescale (see Box 1.15).

This is a particular model, of exemplary good practice, which may not be suitable for all circumstances or all corporate training budgets. The outline stages, however, provide guidance on how manager development can make sure of a common competence model:

- Adoption of an accepted model: and the training of staff to be able to use it.
- Assessment of learners/managers against the model.
- Develop recognition and understanding of the model by the managers.
- Gain acceptance by managers of their assessment profile.
- Individual Action Planning takes place.

The details of each of these stages can be adapted by organisations to

---

Box 1.15 Developing competences

This model of a competence development programme takes managers away from the workplace for two weeks: one week to undertake the audit and then one week at a later stage for feedback and the preparation of the Action Plan. The course is strongly group based.

An alternative model of an intensive one week course for junior managers, covering eight of the competence groups, and utilising role play and simulation to encourage self-analysis and recognition of the competences in action is found in Boyatzis 1982 Appendix C.

suit their own style and the resources available for manager development.

Part Two of this book sets out in detail a range of methods that can be used to help managers to develop competences necessary or desirable for effective performance, using the Management Learning Contract approach.

Summary

In this chapter we have seen that the competence movement represents a particular approach to management recruitment, selection and development.

Competences are relevant qualities and skills that lead to effective job performance. They are related to observable behaviours, so they can be tested and confirmed.

A number of models of manager competences have been developed, and a variety of methods have been employed, including:

- systematic analysis of the skills of highly effective managers and comparison of these profiles with those of less effective colleagues.
- a collection of informed opinions of the skills thought necessary for an effective manager, which are then tested in practice.
- the refinement of an existing generic model for use in a particular organisation.

We have seen that generic models have been developed that may be adapted for particular organisations or for particular jobs. They can also be used as they stand as a means of selection and training for managers who can handle change.

Of the methods used to assess the competences of individual managers, we have seen that the Behavioural Event Interview and Assessment Centre Simulations are those most favoured by specialists, but there are doubts about the effectiveness of these methods in certain situations.

As competences are defined in behaviour and skill terms, it is undoubtedly feasible to train and develop managers to help them to become more competent. We saw a particular example of such a development process.

Exercises

At the end of each chapter of this book there are a number of questions designed to help you to recall and to apply the ideas and techniques set out in the chapter. You will find some answers – or some commentary on the questions – at the end of the book, together with a list of reading references for the chapter.

1.   Two qualities often mentioned in connection with the superior or effective manager are 'Proactivity' and 'Self-Confidence'. What behaviours would you associate with each of these qualities? How would you recognise them if you saw them?

2.   Considering your own organisation: what would be the advantages and what would be the difficulties of using a generic competence model as a basis for management development?

Chapter 2

Competence standards

by Lindsay Mitchell

When you have completed this chapter you should be able to:

- explain how occupational standards describe what is expected of managers at work.
- distinguish between the standards approach to competence and the qualities and skills approach and describe how the two approaches are complementary.
- recognise standards and how they are expressed.
- describe how standards can be used for training and development within organisations.

Introduction

Defining the qualities and skills which individuals require is one approach to trying to improve the effectiveness of the work-force, in this case management. Recently, however, this approach has been criticised as being only a partial solution because it does not consider in sufficient detail what is expected of an individual at work. 'It is like a manufacturer specifying the materials and equipment necessary for production without a precise description of what is going to be produced' (*BSD/ITS 1990*). That is, it does not tell us the outcomes in terms of performance required of managers but rather looks at whether a manager has the likely qualities and skills for the work in question.

The qualities and skills approach to competence assumes that if an individual has certain qualities and skills, he/she will be able to combine these attributes to meet the various demands of their job both now and in the future. 'Superior managers' are those individuals who either have *more* qualities and skills, have the qualities and skills to a greater extent than average performers, or are able to *process* the qualities and skills in a more effective way.

The purpose and uses of the standards approach

The standards approach to competence does not deny that each individual needs qualities, skills, and knowledge in order to be able to perform but it does not see them as the prime means to achieve a competent work-force. Rather it takes the viewpoint that first we must decide what the details of competent performance look like for particular work roles. Essentially the standards approach asks: what expectations do we have of a manager at work both now and in the future?

It does not ask this about a particular manager undertaking a particular job, but any individual who has to carry out that function. The initial focus is not on individuals and the attributes which they possess but on the requirements of the role to be performed (see Box 2.1). The standards approach assumes that for the baseline description of competence, it does not matter which individual undertakes the work. Of key importance are the demands placed on any individual performing that function. Each individual will draw on their own knowledge and skills in order to meet the expectations expressed in the standards.

It is helpful to see the two approaches to competence as complementary ways of looking at the development processes of organisations. The standards describe the outcomes of performance

---

Box 2.1 Competence from different viewpoints

The traditional way of viewing competence, that is as the personal characteristics, either innate or learned, which individuals possess, is a psychological way of looking at the world. Individuals are seen to be the centre of action and the interest is on what one individual as compared to another is able to bring to a situation. Individuals tend to be looked at as entities in their own right rather than as social actors.

Functional analysis and the definition of standards stems more from a sociological viewpoint and uses the concept of role, in this sense a work role. The analogy, if it is not stretched too far, is that of an actor playing a role to an audience and also influenced by others of significance, such as other actors, the author, the director, etc. The expectations of these other players will all have an effect on the person who is playing the part.

A role exists in a particular setting, in this case that of the organisation, and is defined in relation to other roles and those with whom those playing the role interact. The expectations which surround the performance of a particular role are held by others and also by the person filling the part him/herself. One of the key aspects of roles is the focus which is given to relationships and the view of the individual as part of a larger social setting. The individual is influenced, and to some degree constrained, by the expectations placed upon him/her. In work roles managers often have greater freedom of action than others, but they too (like any other worker) must deliver what is expected of them.

expected of any manager performing a particular work role. They are a quality specification for the people which the organisation employs. Like any specification of quality, they provide benchmarks against which management performance is assessed. That is, they give descriptions of what a manager should be aiming at, and consistently trying to achieve, as he/she undertakes particular work functions.

The standards provide organisations with quality specifications for the people whom they employ. The standards can be used, among other things, to:

- specify the requirements of a particular post, i.e. as a job specification.
- detail the objectives of training and development programmes.
- evaluate whether people are providing what the organisation requires of them.
- evaluate development and training to determine whether it is meeting organisational needs.
- monitor and identify personnel requirements and shortages.

Defining standards of competence

Functional analysis – starting points

Occupational standards, and the method of defining them (functional analysis[*]), have developed from a belief that the way to ensure training is linked to the demands of work through making those demands explicit. This focus should be as much, if not more, on emerging trends and changes as it is on the here and now. This will help ensure that training is forward looking and invests in the future competence of the work-force.

The work which has been undertaken in standards development is broader than management although this is seen as of prime importance (*Dept. of Employment 1981*). The UK Standards Development Programme has the long-term aim of detailing the standards required for all work roles (see Box 2.2).

Standards as a definition of work demands are not achieved by focussing on atomised tasks which an individual has to carry out but through looking at broader functions or purposes. This broader focus is essential because of the changing nature of work.

---

[*]Standards are determined by using a process called 'functional analysis' developed by BSD Ltd and now widely used in the UK standards programme.

Box 2.2 The UK Government's Standards Development Programme and its relationship to National Vocational Qualifications

The Government's Standards Development Programme, for which responsibility rests with the Training Agency, has as its key purpose the development of occupational standards across all industry. This follows the publication of the New Training Initiative in 1981, which stated that the UK must 'develop training . . . to agreed standards . . . appropriate to the jobs available . . .'

The 1980s saw a gradual expansion of the TA's role in developing occupational standards as a basis for training, which was further underlined by the establishment of the National Council for Vocational Qualification (NCVQ) in 1986. NCVQ's remit is to establish a framework of vocational qualifications based on occupational standards in order to rationalise and reform the rather confusing proliferation of awards of the past.

In order to ensure that vocational education and training, and the related qualifications, are truly based on the demands of employment, a number of Lead Bodies have been established, facilitated by the Training Agency. Lead Bodies are designed to represent employer, employee and education interests and develop, monitor and maintain nationally recognised occupational standards for their particular section of industry.

Once standards have been established and agreed by industry, the Lead Body agrees on a method of assessment and how it will be implemented with one or more Awarding Bodies. The assessment format agreed should meet the criteria of assessment practice laid down by the NCVQ. Lead Bodies also have a continuing role in ensuring that the standards and their related assessment systems continue to reflect the industry's demands.

There are currently nearly 200 Lead Bodies in existence which vary in size, constitution and the occupational area which they cover. Some, like the Lead Body for management and supervisory staff, the National Forum for Management Education and Development (NFMED) are cross-sectoral and look at the work roles undertaken by a particular group of workers. Others, such as the Care Sector Consortium (CSC), are sectorally based but broad in focus. The CSC covers all care sector activities for the Health Service, Social Services and private and voluntary sectors. Finally there are Lead Bodies who have a more restricted remit and focus on a particular industry or group of workers, such as the British Brush Manufacturers Association.

It is currently too early in the development process to evaluate the impact which Lead Bodies, the development of standards and the related National Vocational Qualifications will have on training, both in-company and in the public sector, and whether this will lead to a significant improvement in the competence of the work-force.

Work study and work measurement are based on a supposition that each work operation can be sub-divided and broken down into small tasks for which specific skills training can then take place. In the modern economy such tasks are disappearing and where they are necessary they are performed by machines. There is an increasing need for a thinking and flexible work-force, not least at management level

Standards are designed to make all these demands explicit and consequently to capture all aspects of work, both those which are related to specific tasks and those which are 'softer' (*Spencer 1983*). Functional analysis does this by looking at the purpose of any actions because it is these purposes which determine the outcomes to be achieved, i.e. the expectations placed on an individual.

Functional analysis stems from a perspective that:

- all aspects of work should be covered in the analysis frame,
- the outcomes should be as much determined by future requirements as by the needs of the present day, and
- the reason for developing standards is to improve the quality of the work-force.

One of the key tools which is used when undertaking a functional analysis is the Job Competence Model (*Mansfield and Mathews, 1985*). This provides a mechanism for ensuring that the resulting standards reflect all aspects of the work role and are broad in focus rather than merely task-based.

The Job Competence Model highlights four components of occupational competence which are to do with:

- *technical skills:* the traditional 'product skills' which enable people to achieve tangible outcomes.
- *task management:* the ability to manage a number of often competing demands and co-ordinate all aspects of the job. (This is, of course, the key to management.)
- *contingency management:* the ability to manage variance and contingency at work – to restore systems when things go wrong, to diagnose and solve problems and to adapt quickly to new systems and tasks.
- *role or job environment:* the ability to manage, co-ordinate and control the external interface with the environment, including health and safety, interaction with others (workers and customers), manage and improve quality and standards and work in different environmental cultures.

By using the Job Competence Model as a starting point for, and framework of, the analysis, and also for evaluating the standards as they are produced, functional analysis aims to capture all aspects of work in terms of the outcomes expected of a manager.

Another major aspect of functional analysis is the use to which it puts *iteration* which it employs as an integral part of the analysis process. That is, the analysis proceeds by recommending options about purposes and functions which are reviewed, tested and refined in the light of later discussions and findings. This means that the entire process is one of constant reflection and refinement, as one might expect when the aim is to describe reality. During the analysis the model is not fixed but held in a constant state of 'draft' until there is sufficient agreement that the descriptions do reflect what is expected in real life.

Iteration is also a useful mechanism for ensuring that the standards are updated as the need arises and as there are changes in work requirements. As changes arise they can be incorporated into the overall model in a consistent way by reflecting the impact on the whole model and tracking through to make which adjustments are necessary. This is achieved in a similar way to modifying or altering a production or delivery system where the extent of the change is determined by the effect which the alteration has on other functioning parts.

Functional analysis – process

The stages below describe the process which is used, but should be considered against the background of the Job Competence Model and the use of iteration discussed above.

The process for functional analysis is:

- first, select the occupational area of interest and decide its key purpose in terms of the overall outcomes to which all are working. This will involve discussions with a number of job holders until a working definition is arrived at. The occupational areas can be as large as a whole industrial sector, such as the Health Service, can be focussed on particular work roles, such as management, or may be as small as particular job titles, e.g. works supervisor.
- second, working from the key purpose define the outcomes which help that purpose to be achieved. This is usually carried out in workshop session with job holders probing into the ways in which they characterise their work and the manner in which the functions can be split. Preferably the workshops consist of some participants who are recognised as forward thinking and will be able to inform the work by concentrating on the emerging trends and developments.

- third, continue the process, reflecting back and re-drafting as necessary, until the statements of expectations which are produced are undertaken by an individual or a number of individuals and the descriptions would allow assessment of that individual to take place.
- fourth, test out the definitions with a wider audience to ensure that there is common agreement with the results and modify where necessary.
- fifth, start planning the routes by which the standards will be implemented dependent on the purpose to which they will be put.

The procedure follows a systematic, agreed framework which determines what the resulting picture of the standards should look like (see Box 2.3). It is also inherently logical in that the key purpose, which is the overall definition for the start of the process, must cover all the functions which are described below it.

Box 2.3 An example of the structure of occupational standards

This diagram shows the basic framework of standards. This is also the structure which vocational qualifications must take if they are to meet the criteria of NCVQ. The number of stages there are in the breakdown before units of competence are reached is dependent on the starting point of the analysis. For example, if the starting point is a job title, units are likely to be reached at the first level of breakdown as illustrated here. If the starting point is the key purpose of an organisation, there may be many higher levels before this.

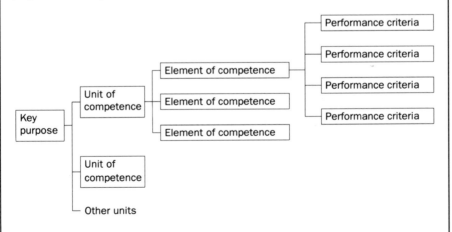

(In practice there will be many more units and elements in a qualification. This diagram simply shows the structure of units, elements and performance criteria.)

We identify the overall key purpose of the area we are looking at. So for example, a key purpose of management may be:

- to maintain and improve the services provided by the organisation,

then we identify the different things which have to happen for that to take place, such as,

- establish and maintain the supply of resources to the organisation,
- implement changes in services, products and systems,

then we describe the outcomes by which we would know a manager is performing the job successfully, such as,

- communications with suppliers are conducted in a manner which promotes goodwill and trust,
- estimates, tenders and quotations are prepared on time, comply with organisational policies and contain enough information for the customer to make a decision.

A manager is matched against the 'ideal' of the standards to see whether he/she as an individual is able to achieve the standards set. The individual either meets the standards and is therefore deemed competent, or fails to meet the standards and is not yet competent. The actual descriptions of occupational competence lie outside the individual as benchmarks (criteria) against which individuals are measured.

Later in this chapter we will look at how these criteria may be used as the focus for development and training. Let us first, however, consider the points which we have covered so far.

- The standards approach to competence differs from the qualities and skills approach in that it defines the expectations of any manager performing a work role by describing the outcomes of performance which are expected.
- The standards do not deny that qualities, skills and knowledge are important, but consider that these are supplementary issues which follow on from describing work role expectations.
- The standards are quality specifications for the work-force and may be applied to any occupational group within it.
- The standards provide a framework against which the development of all the work-force can be seen against current and emerging organisational objectives and requirements.

National work in the UK on generic standards for managers

As part of the UK government's push to improve the quality of the work-force, a large-scale programme of the work (the Standards Development Programme) has been established to identify the standards of competence required by all occupational sectors. One of the key parts of this programme is the work being undertaken jointly by the National Forum for Management Education and Development (NFMED) and the Training Agency (TA).

This project managed by NFMED has been looking at the competences required of 'most managers all of the time', no matter what their area of employment (*NFMED 1990*). The work will provide a source of information for decision makers on the standards required by managers in a general sense. It will be available for organisations to draw on for their own specific purposes and to use to improve the development of people which takes place within the organisation.

NFMED also intend that the standards will provide a unifying framework for management development courses and the assessment and accreditation of individuals for these courses in the future. Essentially this will mean that if an individual has a qualification, which is based on the nationally recognised standards, the certificate will testify to the fact that he/she has achieved the criteria specified.

As the NFMED model of standards is focussed on the generic aspects of managerial work, there may be a need to supplement the model with additional standards to take account of the particular circumstances of certain jobs. The advantage of using the national standards is that an organisation has a clear relationship to the world at large and particularly the vocational education and training system. The advantage of developing standards which are internal to an organisation is that the standards are able to express that organisation's unique requirements. (*Mathews 1990*)

In the longer term, standards should be available for most of the functions in the economy and organisations will need to undertake little extra work themselves providing that the standards meet the specifications which they require of their personnel. In the shorter term, the degree to which a complete map of standards is available will be dependent on the success of the Standards Development Programme in providing the necessary coverage in a way to which organisations can relate.

As one would expect of any quality specification, the standards need to go into a fairly high level of detail for the actual outcomes expected of a manager to be described. For example, the NFMED project has produced 26 elements of competence (grouped into 9 units of competence which can be viewed as larger chunks) for those working at the level of what may be loosely described as a junior manager. The elements, parcelled into units of competence, are grouped under the four key roles of operations, finance, people and information.

Each of the elements of competence has somewhere between four and ten performance criteria attached to it, which are the descriptions of successful performance.

Some examples of the elements of competence produced by the NFMED project for generic standards of management are given below. You will notice that each follows the same grammatical structure and focusses on purposeful activity. For example, managers need to be able to:

- implement and evaluate changes to services, products and systems.
- monitor and control costs against budgets.
- plan activities and determine work methods to achieve objectives.
- lead meetings and group discussions to analyse problems and make decisions.

A list of all the standards of competence for a manager is obviously fairly long and complex in the detail which is provided. This is because not only does each of the key areas of activity which the manager needs to be able to undertake have to be specified, but also against each of these there is a description of the outcomes specifying the required quality. For the element of competence: *implement and evaluate changes to services, products and systems.*

The performance criteria against which an individual's performance would be assessed are:

- relevant details of implementation plans are communicated in a manner, level and pace appropriate to those concerned and within agreed timescales.
- changes in services, products and systems are monitored in accordance with implementation plans and agreed specifications.
- outcomes of changes are evaluated against expectations and previous service/production records.
- implementation is suitably modified to resolve any problems arising.

These criteria, taken together with the element of competence, provide the specification to which any manager undertaking that function is expected to work. The remainder of this chapter looks at how organisations can make use of the standards in development and training.

How standards can be used for development and training

Processes of development and introduction

The continuing education and development of managers and supervisors is a cornerstone of the future capability of organisations. *Much management training in the past has been dominated by subject areas and an attempt to develop particular skills.*

Occupational standards highlight the outcomes which organisations expect their managers to deliver, such as the co-ordinating of functions and dealing with the unpredictable. *Perhaps of greatest importance, the standards make clear exactly what it is that managers are expected to do, both for those who are actually undertaking the work and those who are appraising their performance, or assisting them to develop their capability.*

Standards can act like a knife to cut through long-held views and help pin down the boundaries and content of exactly what is at issue. This, in itself, may have an impact on managerial performance through clarifying for individuals the actual expectations under which they work and through opening up the discussion on what the organisation demands of them.

There are other more systematic approaches to the use of standards which organisations can adopt and consequently improve the effectiveness of their work-force. The national Standards Development Programmes, run under the auspices of the Training Agency, go through a series of development stages to make sure that the standards are in the best form for their intended use. While the purposes for which individual organisations may want the standards is likely to be somewhat different to how they will be used nationally, the processes have much to offer.

The nationally-recognised standards have three key purposes:

- First, to raise the competence of the UK work-force in the years to come by detailing the standards which are expected in a competitive economy.

- Second, by using the standards as the basis for a unified structure of vocational qualifications – National Vocational Qualifications – to ensure that vocational qualifications are closely linked to the requirements of work.
- Third, by the qualifications, and more importantly the standards upon which they are based, being the driving force (objectives) for vocational education and training.

The national programme tends to adopt the following processes.

- Under the leadership of an 'expert', drafting the standards through consultation with a key group of job holders and their managers, until they are in a form which the group believes is ready for wider consultation.
- Discussion and feedback from a wider group to give further insights, to make sure that good practice is contained and that all angles have been taken into account. This leads to further reflection and refinement of the standards.
- Trialling of the standards in the manner in which it is intended they will be implemented. For the national programme (which is linked to qualifications with an emphasis on assessment of achievement in the work-place) this means giving the standards to the managers/superiors of the job holders and seeing whether they can understand the criteria and interpret them consistently; whether the standards actually do discriminate between those who perform the job as required and those who do not; and evaluating whether the standards embody good practice.

The results of these processes are used both for continual refinement of the standards and to inform the way in which any programme will be implemented.

For companies who are using standards for internal development purposes, the consultation will not need to be so great and there is more likely to be a consensus of purpose and culture. National discussion not only checks the standards are right, although of course this is the primary aim, but also provides a useful forum for all those who will be affected by the standards to reflect and debate the content.

The process is a useful mechanism for:

- achieving consensus on the standards which are sought
- raising the implementation issues and starting to move towards

agreement as to how the standards will best be used eventually
● marketing the advantages which the standards will bring.

While individual organisations are unlikely to want to commit the resources to wide-scale or in-depth consultation, it is worth while considering the benefits which phased implementation can bring in terms of ensuring that the standards actually reflect what happens on the ground and that those involved have a sense of ownership of, and commitment to, what they contain.

Standards as tools for individual development

Assessment of achievement is sought by gathering evidence of performance under the pressures of real work (as far as is possible) and supplementing this by supporting evidence, such as oral questioning. As standards are a quality specification against which individuals are assessed, the extent to which a particular individual matches up to the specification will usually differ from that of another individual. For example, one manager may be good at forecasting trends and developments which impinge on his/her area of responsibility but have difficulty in communicating this information to others in a form of which they can readily make sense and use. The second manager may have got the ongoing monitoring of costs to a fine art but be unable to fully justify why her area is in need of further resources for a development which is crucial to the organisation as a whole.

The standards offer a framework for determining exactly what it is that individuals can, and cannot do, and where developmental effort needs to be focussed. In companies their major use is likely to be in assessing individuals initially and/or continuously and using the results to inform development. This is in contrast to the national programme linked to qualifications, where final decisions on competence for certification purposes will need to be made.

The standards approach, as in all competence approaches, focusses on the individual and suggests that whatever mode of response an organisation uses, this should be tied to improving performance from the individual's current achievements. This takes us away from set courses and curricula, where there has often been an assumption that all those on the course have the same learning needs, to more flexible forms of response. This gives a related shift in the trainer's primary role away from implementing training courses to assisting in the assessment of learning objectives and needs, the design of learning and development programmes, and evaluation and review of the results of these (*Stanton 1989*).

Hearing this, our first thought tends to be that the resource implications of such a move are enormous. However, there is another side to the story. With a shift to more individualised assessment of learning needs and wants, there is also a parallel shift to the individual taking more responsibility for their own development. Learning programmes, particularly for staff who are in post and who wish to upgrade or update their skills, may require little, if any, formal training. The learning process largely may be one of self-development and self-appraisal. The cost, which is likely to be an investment for the organisation if the individual achieves the objectives (linked to the standards), will be in the individual negotiation and discussion which takes place rather than an increase in formal training inputs.

Organisations can introduce competence-standards in a number of ways. Three scenarios are presented below each of which uses standards but with different commitments to the individuals within the organisation. A company could:

- institute a formal appraisal system based on the standards, use this as a strict measure of whether individuals are achieving or not and take the action believed to be necessary if it is found that someone does not meet one or more of the criteria. This means that responsibility for development is effectively taken away from the individual and placed with the organisation for it to decide the remedial action.

- encourage individual managers to use the standards for self-appraisal purposes and leave it up to the individuals whether they seek development to improve their practice in these areas or not. This leaves the responsibility with the individual and leaves the organisation none the wiser as to whether its work-force is meeting the quality of operations which is demanded of them.

- set up a process by which individual managers in consultation with mentors, either their line manager, a trainer or a combination of the two, assess their areas of strengths and weaknesses and then agree a programme of development towards the objectives set in the standards. The responsibility for the development rests jointly with both the individual and the organisation. Both make commitments to improving performance. The one through self-development, honesty and reflection. The other through support and the provision of the necessary and agreed resources.

The purpose of standards is to improve the quality of the work-force. It is up to companies to decide, if they are to use standards, the implementation methods which would best support their purposes.

Summary

In this chapter we have seen that the standards approach to competence, derived through the process of functional analysis, represents a particular approach to the development of the work-force, and in this context to management. This view sees competence as the performance of work roles in real working environments, and the expectations which are placed on any individual performing a work role.

Individuals are matched against the expected outcomes of performance specified in the standards to assess their particular learning and development needs. The standards approach to competence can be viewed as complementary to the qualities and skills approach as it helps determine an individual's learning objectives and clearly relates these to organisational requirements.

Organisations can decide to use the standards in a variety of ways which give differing degrees of responsibility to those involved. All competence approaches are based on the philosophy that learning should start from the needs and requirements of the learner. The standards approach attempts to define the changes which are taking place in the nature of work and the consequent demands that these place on the work-force in terms of competence.

We are all in the position of constantly having to adapt, improve and develop our performance in order to continue to meet the changing requirements which organisations place upon us. An approach which shares the responsibility for such development between the individual managers and the organisation for which they are working is likely to be one that continues to be effective.

Exercises

1. As standards are a specification of quality for the work-force, what are the different ways in which an organisation could exploit their use?

2. Thinking about the organisation for which you work, if you were to introduce standards what are the uses to which you would put them and how would you phase their implementation?

Part Two

The Management Learning Contract Manual

Chapter 3

Management Learning Contracts

When you have completed this chapter you should be able to:

- describe a Management Learning Contract.
- explain its strengths and uses as a method of management development.
- explain the principles on which it is based.
- distinguish the MLC approach from similar approaches to learning and development.

Freedom with responsibility

A Management Learning Contract is a formal agreement between a manager and a trainer about what the manager will learn and how that learning will be measured. The agreement will also cover the manager's action plan and the resources he/she will need. The agreement is formal in that the terms are set down in writing, and the document is signed.

A simple standard form for the Management Learning Contract covers one sheet of A4, set sideways in landscape format. It contains spaces for the manager to put proposals under the following headings:

- *Goal.* What is the contract all about? What might be its title?
- *Objectives.* What knowledge and/or skills do you intend to gain?
- *Activities.* How are you going to achieve your objectives? What tasks, projects, experiences, exercises will you do?
- *Resources.* Resources which will be used – books, audiotapes, films, people to be contacted, help you might need.
- *Assessment.* What evidence will you show to assess your learning? What criteria will be used to ensure this learning is satisfactory?

There are spaces for contact telephone numbers, a completion date, the signature of the parties to the contract and the date of signing. (*NRMC 1987*)

The subject of the contract – what the manager will learn – is a matter of individual choice. Ideally, it is a skill which the manager wishes to acquire to improve his/her job performance, a job competence which needs to be developed, a technique which should be improved upon.

Since 1986, trainers from the Northern Regional Management Centre have negotiated and assessed Management Learning Contracts with managers working in organisations as varied as local authorities and petro-chemical companies, mass manufacturers and retailers, project engineers and finance companies and police forces, and many diverse learning needs have been accommodated within the MLC method. A brief survey of the broad areas of learning undertaken by these managers would have to mention the more common interpersonal skills – Interviewing (Recruitment, Appraisal and Disciplinary), Counselling, Training, Chairing Meetings, Negotiating and Persuading, Making Presentations, Delegating – the various contracts that have involved finance skills and techniques, the large numbers of people who have taken their first steps into the foreign country of Information Technology, the Self Management MLCs (Time and Stress Management, Confidence Building), and the broad church of Miscellany which includes learning how to work particular organisational systems, learning and applying relevant legislation, learning parts of foreign languages, and more.

Box 3.1   What is management?

The foreign language examples have arisen only occasionally, and usually because the manager is in contact with European visitors from time to time. The first time a participant on one of our programmes asked to learn parts of a foreign language, however, it was because he was going to spend six months on a placement in the South Yemen, and he wished to learn some Yemeni Arabic.

An officer of the Business and Technician Education Council queried what this had to do with management. We pointed out that it was difficult to manage people without being able to communicate with them.

Information Technology is another popular area, and where this is used to analyse information relevant to managing – about plans or operations – it seems completely appropriate for this to fall within the scope of a Management Learning Contract.

This is only a brief survey and disguises the fact that no two MLCs are exactly alike, and even two MLCs in the same broad area are likely to exhibit significantly different features in goal, assessment measures and action plan. This diversity is due to factors basic to the development process:

- different organisational styles and expectations.
- different job roles, making different demands.

- different individual needs for development.
- the necessity to express precise learning objectives and assessment measures in the contract.

So, for example, three people may choose, one after another, to improve their time management skills and, through discussion with a trainer, agree on three quite different contracts.

Box 3.2 Time management

Time management is often selected as an MLC area, perhaps because a range of different problems at the personal, interpersonal and organisational level result in symptoms of time-pressure and the perceived need for better individual organisation. A time management exercise or an MLC can be a good method of diagnosing actual problem areas and real development needs (see *Boak and Stephenson 1987*).

Approaches to improved time management are of three general types:

- the logging approach, which seeks a very detailed analysis of activity over a short period of time. This may be all activity or only suspected problem areas (e.g. how much time do I spend in meetings?). The detailed log is analysed against a set of priorities; areas of waste are identified. The manager then sets about improving the position in respect of waste in one, two or three areas.
- the planning approach which requires the manager to make monthly and detailed daily plans for the period of the MLC, to set priorities against planned activities, and to analyse completion and non-completion at the end of each day.
- specific problem-solving approaches, in which the manager has already identified an aspect of the problem which he/she wants to tackle: a more effective means of handling appointments, or paperwork, or team meetings, where the skills to be developed are quite specific and may have little to do with the traditional organising-type skillls usually associated with time management: being assertive about refusing requests is an example.

Although time management is a commonly chosen MLC area, there is a range of possible contract agreements, with different objectives and different assessment measures.

See also Case Study 3 in Chapter 10 below.

There are evident advantages in the Management Learning Contract approach, and the confirmation of this has been the expression of satisfaction by learners/managers and their employers and the increasing use of the MLC method by client organisations. To some extent, each individual experience speaks for itself, but some features of the approach may be identified as contributing to its success:

- *Flexibility.* Learning Contracts can be used to address any learning area. Within a particular training or development programme the scope may be more limited, but it should still be more wide-ranging than any choice of pre-packaged options.
- *Participation.* The individual learner/manager participates in devising the MLC (in fact, as we shall see, he/she should take the lead role). This has a tremendous effect on motivation. The relevant line manager, or mentor, can also participate in devising and assessing the contract, and this involvement is also helpful.
- *Relevance.* The MLC can use real job issues, real work problems and achieve real development. The qualities of flexibility and participation, used to the full, virtually guarantee relevance.
- *Structure.* The formal nature of the agreement provides a firm structure to guide and support each individual contract. Surrounding the contract itself there should be a structure of rights and obligations, freedoms and responsibilities, so the individual learner knows what is possible and what is expected.

Box 3.3 Testimonials

Testimonials to the Management Learning Contract approach focus on the obvious features: the relevance, the availability of help in tackling real problems, the achievement of real development.

The line managers of learners – who are able to take a more detached view – often testify to the acceleration in development, because of the focus on learning. 'Frank learned skills he would have had to learn anyway, but in a shorter time than I would have expected.'

Line managers are more likely to comment on a change in attitude – to one that is more positive, whereas learners are more likely to reflect on what has happened in terms of a gain in confidence, or in self-confidence.

These benefits are felt when the MLC approach is used correctly by the two (or three) parties to the contract, and each play their necessary role. The learner/manager must be prepared to learn, must be willing to take the initiative in proposing terms of the contract, and must be prepared to see it through.

The trainer must be prepared to listen, to question, to summarise and to support: it will usually fall to the trainer to introduce the approach, too, and arrange the logistics.

The organisation – represented by the learner's boss or department head – must be prepared to allow some time and latitude from the business of production today to allow the staff to develop to ensure production tomorrow, and should be prepared to acknowledge the achievements of successful developers.

Foundations

There are a number of common-sense reasons to explain the success of Management Learning Contracts. The approach is founded on certain basic principles of learning and development. It is helpful to make these explicit to users – the trainers, the learner/managers and the line managers who will be involved.

The Learning Circle

The principles and use of the Learning Circle will be well known to most trainers. Since its promotion by David Kolb (1976) and Peter Honey and Alan Mumford (1982), the Circle has made regular appearances on training and development programmes. Perhaps we can see in its rise and popularity the same forces that have pushed to prominence competence – as opposed to book learning and the mastery of theory.

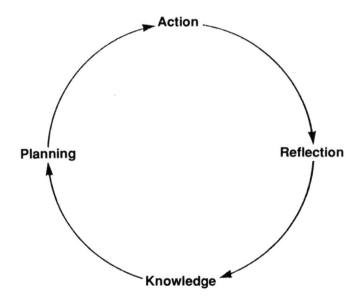

Figure 3.1 The Learning Circle

According to Kolb, Honey and Mumford, people only acquire skills (and, we might add, competences) by undertaking four different types of activity, represented on the circle as Action, Reflection, Knowledge, Planning (Fig 3.1).

It is difficult to know where to break into the circle to explain the development of a specific skill: let us suppose that I am a junior manager, in charge of others for the first time and grappling with difficulties of delegation. We can begin with ACTION (I delegate, or fail to delegate) and there are consequences of this, which may range from outstanding success to absolute failure.

If I am trying to develop my skill here, and repeat the successes and avoid future failures, I should REFLECT on what has happened – What did I do right? What did I do wrong?

Perhaps from this, some principles will emerge (the KNOWLEDGE component). They may be general theories, they may be rules of thumb. They may be augmented by books I seek out on delegation, or information from lectures I attend, or the advice of friends and colleagues. (Conventional management education and training is very strong on the knowledge component.)

The next occasion which calls for delegation should cause me to do some PLANNING, and to consider which of my general principles are applicable in this particular case, and how it should be approached.

I may go round the Circle many times before I become truly skilled as a delegator.

Box 3.4 The Learning Circle

The description of the Learning Circle as action – reflection – knowledge – planning – action owes more to Peter Honey and Alan Mumford than to David Kolb. The reflection and knowledge (conceptualisation) stages are virtually the same in both models, but then Kolb prefers 'active experimentation' for planning and his action stage is more about using the skill on a regular basis in a real life setting. This appears to expand the time frame of progress around the circle.

The Learning Circle emphasises that the development of skill is more than the acquisition of knowledge: some action should also be undertaken, and then evaluated.

The Management Learning Contract is a particularly suitable vehicle for skill development in that:

- a specific skill area can be identified for development for each person.
- specific actions can be agreed with each person, depending on his/her needs and the opportunities available.
- the relevant supporting knowledge base can be identified.
- a structure for reflection on the experience, and for action planning can be agreed.

Box 3.5 The knowledge base

All skills have a knowledge component. This may be an element of theory or guidance on how to behave or what to aim to achieve, which might be gleaned from books or gained from discussion with others. It may also consist of feedback about one's current level of skill, and priority areas for improvement. A questionnaire or a logging approach can provide a method of gathering and organising this information.

So, for example, the manager who wishes to improve his counselling skills might first of all be guided to some reading that will help him to clarify in his own mind what 'counselling skills' are, and then to assess his own performance to see which of these skills are most in need of improvement, before beginning the actual skill development.

To take another example, the manager who wishes to improve her presentation skills might be introduced to a number of techniques, and guidance on how to use them, before beginning the actual skill development by practice.

The principles of the Learning Circle also have important lessons for the construction of an MLC, and can help the learner and the trainer to agree a series of activities that will lead to a genuine development of competence.

Staged improvement

The second founding principle of the MLC approach is that the development of all skills takes place in stages. As a novice to delegation, for example, I am unlikely to become expert in the course of three or four weeks. I can, however, improve on my initial level of ability – I can become a *better* delegator if not an expert. The only difficulty in this case may be defining the stages and agreeing clear targets. With Information Technology, or Financial Analysis the definition of stages is quite simple. With other skill areas the definitions may be more elusive, the graduation from one stage to another less well established or clear cut, but development does remain gradual, and takes time to show itself.

The MLC method relies upon establishing attainable, clearly defined targets over relatively short periods of time. Small changes in behaviour may be the aim, or to climb two, three or four steps up the scale from the present level of skill, towards greater competence (see Box 3.6).

Box 3.6 The historical roots

As a postscript to this section on the foundations of the MLC approach, Mac Stephenson has traced the roots of Management Learning Contracts back to the early Empiricists, by way of studies of Adult Learning, Independent Study and Experiential Learning.

In particular, four elements are emphasised:

- *participation* from studies of adult learning,
- *relevance* from studies of cognition,
- *discovery*, and
- *consequences of behaviour* from early studies of experiential learning.

(*Stephenson 1990; also Hartley 1987, and Keeton 1981*)

Contracts and competences

In the first two chapters we considered competences in two different ways:

- *competences as skills,* anchored to descriptions of behaviour.
- *competence standards,* defining and describing what a manager is expected to produce.

Both of these approaches to competence concern behaviour at work, and both go to some lengths to define the behaviour in such a way that it can be recognised.

Management Learning Contracts provide a means of helping a manager to develop appropriate competences.

- *Individual needs for development* differ from manager to manager. The competence models – whether generic or specific to a company or to a particular job role – or simply the descriptions of competence in particular areas, enable an analysis and a definition of individual needs.

If a generic model is used, the definition is likely to be more detailed, more thoroughly researched, and more widely accepted than any previous definitions of skill or performance have been.

If a company model is used, at least the acceptance within that organisation should be widespread.

- *Management Learning Contracts* support the establishment of personal learning targets by diverse individuals. The need for clear definition of the targets can be met, or assisted by, the competence statements. The realism of the manager's plan to develop the competences is a product of the MLC method, as we shall see.
- *Developing skills* in the work environment, within the challenges of the job, is a particular feature of the MLC approach that sits well with the aims of the competence movement. The initial flexibility of the approach enables an adaptation to the features of a specific – perhaps unique – management situation: the detail of the written contract enables a clear, precise definition of what is to be achieved and how that will be assessed, sufficient to measure against a general standard of competence, or to compare with the achievements of managers in different jobs.

These benefits are not experienced automatically, as soon as Management Learning Contracts are brought into use. At the heart of the MLC method is an interaction between two (or more) individuals, who are sometimes discussing matters both sensitive and important. The success of the method is not simply a matter of mechanics, but of skill. It is not enough just to use Management Learning Contracts: they must be used thoughtfully, carefully, skilfully, to be effective.

Contractual relations

In its general appearance, the Management Learning Contract method is not unique. It belongs to a family of methods of learning, development and appraisal, and there are the resemblances that one might expect between relations.

Contract learning

Learning Contracts have been used successfully in other contexts, particularly in the USA, on undergraduate courses. In this context the majority of contracts are about what specific subject area the student will research, the resources to be used and the nature of the paper that will be written to show understanding (see Box 3.7).

Box 3.7 Learning Contracts

In particular, the Learning Contract has been used extensively at Empire State College, the State University of New York, where undergraduates agree contracts in subjects such as Economics, Business and Society, Industrial Psychology, Marketing, Legal Studies, etc. The contract method is used to negotiate student choice within broad topic areas, to contribute to the attainment of a degree.

Student attitudes to the use of contracts at Empire State are very positive.

(Knowles 1975)

Many of these contracts are about acquiring and using knowledge and demonstrating conceptual skills, whereas the dynamic of their siblings, the Management Learning Contracts, is towards developing and exercising a wider range of competences, skill-orientated and relevant to job performance.

Action planning

A variety of approaches to individual action planning for development are close relatives to MLCs. They fall into two categories: those in which action plans are discussed and agreed, and those in which the lone individual is guided and encouraged to complete an action plan.

An example of the former was described in Chapter 1. Typically there is some diagnosis, or structured self-diagnosis, of areas for development, followed by guidance on the construction of an action plan for self-improvement. Where this tends to differ in particular from an MLC is in the lack of focus on assessment measures, and on the process of joint assessment.

There are a number of examples of the guided solo action plan, as many thoughtful writers over the years have understood that their words will bear more fruit if readers are gently led from a passive state of absorbing ideas into an active state of putting them into practice. Those closest to MLCs in appearance encourage the setting of targets and the assessment of results; those more distantly related provide detailed and down-to-earth suggestions about actions the reader might take.

Box 3.8 Actions Plans

A format for self-assessment and targeting improvement is set out in *A Manager's Guide to Self-Development* by Pedler, Burgoyne and Boydell (1978), and this is complemented by a series of suggested activities related to the self-assessment and the action plan.

Box 3.8 continued

Woodcock and Francis (1975) provide an alternative approach to self-analysis through a heavily coded questionnaire, followed up with a series of suggested activities for self-development.

Honey and Mumford (1982) provide suggestions for practical activities to strengthen approaches to learning that their self-analysis questionnaire may reveal to be in need of development.

Action learning

One of the new approaches to training and development in the 1970s was Action Learning.

Key features of action learning are:

- a focus upon improving the manager's job performance through action and analysis of action in real management situations,
- regular group meetings of learners to discuss the plans, activities and results of each member of the group, which may give rise to
- the group making decisions about what common support is required, such as consultants or visiting speakers on specific subjects.

Box 3.9 Action learning

'The approach of action learning to its mission of helping managers is so simple that it takes any run-of-the-mill professor of management about five years to misunderstand it enough to make conversation at an ordinary meeting of teachers; the big shots, with international reputations to defend, will probably take ten years to attain the order of confusion expected of those who charge a thousand dollars for a one-day stand . . .

'The primary and inescapable obligation of the manager is to run whatever it is he has been appointed to run. Action learning suggests that, since he has to do this in any case, he might just as well find out how he is doing it at the moment and, with what he discovers, try to do it a little better the next day, or next week, or even next year. By asking himself how well things went today, he ought, without great difficulty, to contrive that they go better tomorrow.

'All that I believe I have added to this primary piece of simplicity to turn action learning into programmes of endeavour is what is needed to deal with the questions, "How can the manager know how well he is doing today?" and "How can he then contrive to improve upon it?" In each instance, I suggest that he gets the help and advice of a few other managers, all of whom are honestly bent upon the same purpose, namely to run something better tomorrow by finding out how well or badly they are running it today.' (*Revans 1980*)

The Management Learning Contract approach is a more individual approach than Action Learning, with a greater concentration on the exact plans of the individual learner and less of a concern with the group.

This is a significant difference. MLCs require each individual to design his/her own programme of development and be held responsible for it, whereas the group focus of Action Learning can endanger both individual choice and responsibility.

The MLC approach owes a great deal to the insights and developments of Action Learning, and the group support and discussion at the heart of the social Action Learning approach can be used to support individual progress through an MLC, but the group component is not central, or essential to the use of MLCs.

Management by objectives

The approach of Management by Objectives (MbO) and some other appraisal systems, can be similar to the MLC approach.

Typically, the individual meets with his/her boss (or another senior manager) to discuss and agree targets over the coming year (or six months). Subsequent meetings evaluate performance against these targets. Targets may simply relate to output and production of the main element of the manager's job, or may relate to particular projects or development needs.

The closer the appraisal system resembles the original visions of Management by Objectives, the closer it is related to the MLC approach, because the individual being appraised (the learner) should take the initiative in preparing the terms of the agreement, and much thought should go into performance measures.

Box 3.10 MbO

The early vision of MbO was of a system of agreeing performance targets between a manager and his/her boss, where the initiative in putting forward proposals lay with the manager. The discussion was to proceed in stages, from an initial agreement on priorities (Key Results Areas – KRAs) to proposals and agreements on targets to be achieved and resources to be provided.

An MbO system with these features would:

- benefit from the knowledge each manager has of his/her job area, just as the MLC method relies on the manager's knowledge of his/her own development needs

> **Box 3.10 continued**
>
> • release powerful motivational drives by ensuring that ownership of the proposal rests with the manager, and by precise definition and agreement on how the results will be assessed, as with the MLC method.
>
> (See *Humble 1970*)

There will still, however, be differences. The appraisal system will seldom be about learning, but more often will concentrate on doing: producing output, meeting quantified targets. Where it encounters learning and development there is a tendency to count the inputs – courses attended in particular – rather than attempt to measure the outputs of actual development.

The MLC approach can be used in partnership with appraisal systems – as we shall see, but not every system that involves discussion and agreement uses Management Learning Contracts.

The approach has one other feature in common with each of its four relations: it can easily be mismanaged and thereby discredited – a fate suffered by Management by Objectives in more than one organisation. The Management Learning Contract approach is not a magic wand, bestowing the power to cure all ills upon the trainer who uses it.

For the trainer who introduces it and uses it intelligently, it is a very powerful means of helping managers to develop. It will work in many (but not all) circumstances. It can be used in any skill area, for any level of management.

The rest of this part of the book is about how to introduce the MLC approach and use it most effectively.

The next chapter, 'Preparation', deals with how to introduce Management Learning Contracts to managers in a way that will make them want to play their crucial role with energy and enthusiasm.

'Negotiation', is about what the trainer should be trying to achieve when negotiating a contract, and how to go about that.

'Assessment' gives advice on how to design the performance measures in the contract, and how to use them.

'The role of the trainer' brings together and summarises what the trainer needs to do throughout the whole process, and 'The training triangle' looks at some of the shapes of the relationships between learner, trainer and employer.

Summary

In this chapter, we have introduced the Management Learning Contract: A formal, written agreement between a manager and a trainer about what the manager will learn, how he/she will learn this, what resources will be needed and how the learning will be assessed.

The key advantages of MLCs are:

- *Flexibility* – a wide range of uses.
- *Participation* – which fuels motivation.
- *Relevance* – to real learning needs.
- *Structure* – to support learning and development.

The Management Learning Contract approach is based on simple principles of learning and development:

The *Learning Circle*'s proposition that skills are developed through taking *action*, making time for *reflection*, establishing principles of *knowledge*, and *planning* ahead, helps to justify and structure the MLC approach.

The principle of *staged improvement* establishes each learning contract as a means of developing by degrees – not leaping directly from incompetence to expertise.

We saw that Management Learning Contracts are particularly suitable for competence development in that:

- different individual needs for development can be identified using competence definitions.
- MLCs support individual development and learning.
- learning through work experiences is in particular supported by the MLC method and the competence approach.

There are a number of similar approaches to learning and development: they include:

- (other) learning contracts.
- action planning.
- action learning.
- management by objectives.

Each is related to MLCs, but there are significant differences.

Exercises

1. When a learner and a trainer draw up a Management Learning Contract, they agree on what will be learned. Without looking back through the text, can you say what else they agree upon?

2. The benefits of MLCs are only felt when each of the parties to the contract plays their role correctly. What role is that? Can you suggest what they might do other than play this role?

3. What are the main differences between Action Planning, Management by Objectives and the MLC approach?

Chapter 4

Preparation

When you have completed this chapter you should be able to:

- describe what a trainer should do to prepare a learner/manager for a Management Learning Contract.
- specify the objectives of any presentation introducing managers in your company to the MLC approach.
- explain the strengths and weaknesses of the common methods of self-analysis.
- design a system of priming and diagnosis for your own organisation.

Introduction

The initiative in proposing a particular Management Learning Contract should lie with the manager who will do the learning. Without some guidance and help from the trainer at this stage, however, the MLC approach will take up more time and produce fewer real results than otherwise.

The help that the manager needs can be divided into two types:

- Priming – which means a clear briefing as to the role he/she is expected to play, and some encouragement to do so, and
- Diagnosis – which means some help in selecting a suitable area of knowledge or skill for development.

Priming

At its very least, priming means providing a clear brief to the manager about what he/she is expected to do. At its best, priming inspires the manager to explore areas in which he/she could develop and leads to a clear and thoughtful written proposal for a contract. At its best, priming means that the manager will indeed take ownership of the MLC from the outset, and produce a proposal that he/she is keen to follow through. At its worst, when priming fails, the time and cost necessary to agree an MLC proposal can double, while the noticeable benefit may actually decrease.

Under these circumstances, it is worth taking a careful aim at best practice. Priming can be broken down into three activities:

- explaining what an MLC is and why it is being used.
- building confidence in the MLC approach.
- making clear what the learner/manager has to do.

Best practice priming will deliberately focus on each of these areas. Let us look at each of them in turn.

'What' and 'why'

We saw in the preceding chapter that a Management Learning Contract is essentially a simple agreement between a learner and another person (or persons) which specifies what will be learned, how and when that learning will be measured, what activities will be undertaken to achieve the learning and what resources will be used.

We saw that the MLC approach was based on sound theories of how people learn and develop skills, and on a set of beliefs about the value of learning from real experiences in the work-place.

This, the essence of the 'what' and 'why', should be a central part of the briefing to managers approaching Management Learning Contracts for the first time.

Box 4.1 What is an MLC?

Using a blank copy of a standard contract form is a very good way of introducing a Management Learning Contract.

A basic standard form would include spaces for overall goal, learning objectives, assessment, activities and resources required. This can provide a clear and simple format for explaining what an MLC looks like.

A blank form is better than providing an example of one that has already been completed. Devoid of illustrative – and probably irrelevant – content, the blank form poses questions, invites initiatives.

In particular, it is necessary to focus upon the introspective, learning aspect of the MLC approach. Most managers will be familiar with projects or performance targets and the danger from the outset is that the MLC – which is about learning and personal development – will be confused with a project – which is about doing, or about acquiring and using facts. The skill development aspects of the MLC approach should be emphasised to nip this misapprehension in the bud.

The value of explaining the basis for using Management Learning Contracts has been shown time and time again. In particular, an introduction to the learning circle and its relationship to contract learning can have clearly defined benefits:

- managers are more likely to accept the MLC approach. The theory base is easy to understand, conforms with their experience, and has rational connections with the MLC method.
- managers are more likely to undertake skills-based contracts requiring real action in the work-place – in other words, MLCs that will develop their competence.
- managers are better able to structure the MLC proposal in planning, action, reflection and knowledge terms.
- this approach also helps to answer some questions about assessment that will usually be posed at this point (see Chapter 6).

In addition to explaining the 'what' and the 'why' in general terms it is, of course, desirable to brief managers on the role of Management Learning Contracts in the particular training course, appraisal scheme or development programme in which they are placed. Positive reasons for the use of MLCs must be communicated at this point, or the managers will be disinclined to invest the necessary preparatory effort. We will look at motivation more closely in a moment.

It is advisable for the trainer to brief the learner/manager personally, face-to-face, whether individually or in a group of fellow learners. This is almost always necessary, to generate the required impact to move learners to devise their own contract proposals. Printed material, information and instructions, is useful support but is insufficient by itself.

Confidence and motivation

The second function of priming is to encourage the manager to feel confident in the MLC approach and to be motivated to use it.

Some aspects of motivation will be affected by details of the particular scheme: for example, are people being invited to use MLCs or compelled to do so? What are the consequences of success or failure?

Motivation generally is enhanced by:

- clearly placing responsibility for taking the initiative with the learner/manager, and
- specifying clear targets to be met (a proposal, in a particular form, by a certain date),
- helping the learner/manager to clarify what can be learned, and what should be learned (through the diagnostic process, see below).

Box 4.2 Recognising success

One large company enhanced the motivation of the managers undertaking a series of Management Learning Contracts by recognising success in a number of ways:

- the line manager of each participant was personally involved in the negotiation and assessment of each contract.
- the programme began and ended with a short residential period, and both the launch and the conclusion were attended by a senior manager from the Personnel Department (because that department was in charge of providing the training).
- the conclusion of the programme included a presentation by each member of the programme about what he/she had learned, to fellow learners, senior trainers and the relevant line manager.

Success on the programme was subsequently recognised as a necessary prerequisite for attaining a certain grade of management within the company.

This is an advanced example of a company prepared to invest in training, with a history of management development.

On a more modest scale, the involvement of line managers, the presence of senior managers, and some form of pleasant expenditure (in this case the residential element) indicate an interest and support on the part of the company that always provides some boost to the motivation of the individual managers.

Nevertheless, managers will often approach their first MLC with a degree of trepidation and doubt. This may not be apparent to the person providing the briefing, but it is safe to assume that a little time can be well spent on building confidence in:

- *the method*: some examples of the successes achieved by using MLCs are worth as much as the rational basis on which the method is built (see Box 4.3).
- *the potential*: an emphasis on the ability of everyone to learn new skills can provide or reinforce positive attitudes towards development. It can be too easy for us to think of firm, unchanging lines that separate things we can do from 'things we are no good at' (see Box 4.4).
- *the challenge*: confidence also comes from realising that an MLC is about staged improvement.

The best analogy is a flight of stairs in an office building. At the foot of the stairs on the ground floor is total ignorance of the skill area – financial analysis, or negotiation skills, or information technology or

---

Box 4.3 Success stories

Your own scheme will soon accumulate success stories you can recount in detail and will be proud to talk about. In the meantime you are welcome to talk about some of these genuine achievements:

- the manager who carried out a learning contract to learn some basic Arabic when his company put him on placement in the Middle East for six months. His success in his aim was attested by a bilingual colleague and assessment of an audiotape by a specialist linguist.

- a senior production manager completed a time management and a stress management learning contract and testified that he had learned to go home earlier in the evening, to use his evenings and weekends to good effect with his wife and family and that his work rate had actually improved. By planning his time and refusing to be rushed into crisis management by people around him, he was being more productive and he was also able to be more relaxed.

- the manager of a section providing servicing and repairs to certain consumer goods, in search of a clearer understanding of the company's financial systems, discovered an error in the company's invoicing system that was costing an estimated £65,000 per annum.

- a newly-appointed first-line manager of a team in a computer services area said that he had learned more about counselling skills in two months than he might have done in two years without the concentration, the focus and the motivation of the Management Learning Contract. His boss agreed.

- one manager undertook an assertiveness contract that was almost entirely agreed between his line manager and a trainer, with occasional requests for confirmation from the learner, which he meekly provided. The MLC was assessed at a meeting which began with the trainer saying 'Well, as I understand it, we're here to get a progress report on this contract and we're looking for completion in a month's time'. He got no further. The manager interrupted him, stated that in fact the MLC was complete and proceeded to run the rest of the meeting.

---

whatever. At the head of the stairs on the top floor is complete mastery. An individual learning contract may progress me from the foot of the stairs on the ground floor up one flight – or half a flight. Or, if I am already on the third floor, we may agree that I will aim to finish the MLC on the fourth.

So by undertaking an MLC in financial analysis (or negotiation skills, etc.) I am not proposing to hold myself up as an expert at the end, but simply aiming to improve on my present level of skills – whatever that level is.

Box 4.4 The natural

The 'natural ability' argument can dictate the response to new technology ('I'm no good at computing'), finance ('I'm no good at numbers'), and other technical areas of management, but tends to focus on interpersonal skills ('I'm no good at negotiating', etc.).

The 'I'm no good at . . .' position is essentially a static one ('I want to learn how to . . .' is the corresponding active one).

The more thoughtful aspect of the natural ability argument is based on the observation that some people are better at leading/negotiating/teamwork, etc. than others. Is it, then, possible for those others to be effective leaders/expert negotiators/good team members?

My response is that:

- most people can learn quite difficult skills to some degree (driving a car, using a costing system, communicating in a foreign language, etc.).
- nearly all people can improve their skills in areas of deficiency or needs. (I may not become an expert negotiator, a fluent speaker of German, or a charismatic leader, but I can develop my skills – of bargaining, German or leadership a piece at a time.)

Emphasising this fact has had a marked effect on motivation and confidence. The challenge becomes realistic (see Chapter 9).

- *disclosure*: the manager's confidence is also boosted in most cases by those around him/her taking a positive, honest approach to skills, strengths and weaknesses. In an atmosphere where an admission of weakness is as a confession to sin there will be few honest self-evaluations, but if a learner/manager can see that it is quite acceptable to set out to improve certain skills there is more chance of an honest and accurate appraisal (see Box 4.5).

Obviously, the trainer who is providing the briefing must take into account the working environment of the learner/manager when encouraging disclosure. People other than the trainer will determine the degree of disclosure which is 'safe' – particularly the learner/manager's boss, and his/her colleagues in the work-place, as well as follow learners – but the trainer can have some influence here.

- *the people*: confidence comes from knowing one is in safe hands. Experienced trainers will communicate the fact that they have used these methods before: new hands should rely on the past success of the method, make sure they get all the details correct, and exude an air of quiet competence.

Box 4.5 Unforgivable sins

In most companies there are degrees of inadmissibility of weakness.

Even in highly task-orientated companies it is okay to confess to the need for more knowledge about how other parts of the company work. This is called 'Business Awareness', and the lack of it can be blamed on other people, for not sharing the information, and on the fact that my section has been asked to produce 150 per cent for the last six months.

Next in many companies, is information technology. Depending on the level of penetration it may be okay to want to start from scratch, or it may be a case of wanting to learn how to handle particular types of information on the computer.

About the same level of venial sin is the new technical area I have just taken over – I've just moved into marketing/personnel/technical services and I need to acquire a working knowledge of the techniques quickly.

To the junior managers who have just acquired responsibility for recruitment or appraisal and/or for giving major presentations, and so on, the novelty of the responsibility can sanction the desire to take on a contract in this area.

It is the manager who has been in charge of a team for years who finds it most difficult to focus on developing team-skills.

In an unsympathetic task-orientated company, the atmosphere conspires with the personal difficulty – often to prevent managers improving the skills they need most.

Once more all may not be in the trainer's control: if others are involved – the learner's line manager, or an appointed mentor, fellow learners or work colleagues – then their attitudes will affect the individual's confidence for good or ill.

Overall, at this stage of priming it is important to remember that managers are not entirely rational, logical, trusting individuals. If they were, they would be no good as managers. As well as hearing explanations, they need to be persuaded, motivated and (here and there) reassured: other people have done this, and it works; you can do it, if you want to; no one's perfect, we can all improve: in the end, it's up to you.

The manager's role

We have briefed the manager on the MLC method; we have paid some attention to matters of motivation and confidence. It is also essential to provide a clear picture of what we want the manager to do.

In particular, we can predict and pre-empt questions from managers about:

- the subject of the MLC. How much choice do they have? Is it a completely free choice? (See Box 5.1 in the next chapter.) Are they expected to consult with someone – for example, their own manager? Are there any methods of self-diagnosis they are expected to use? Are they bound by the results of these diagnoses?
- the timing. When do they produce the proposal? How much preparation time do they have? How long will they have to complete the MLC – i.e. how 'big' is it?
- the format. What should their proposal look like? What headings, or prepared forms should they use?
- the people. Who will agree the proposal? Who will assess the completed contract?

Box 4.6 Timing

Approaches to timing will naturally depend upon the particular scheme of which the MLC is a part.

One scheme, operated variously by NRMC, two regions of British Gas and the Northern Provincial Councils, provides for priming two months before the deadline date for agreeing the MLC. The intervening two months is partly taken up with common, foundation studies, but there are also activities the manager is recommended to undertake to devise a proposal. The MLC is scheduled to run for six to eight weeks.

A second scheme, suitable for short course work, is for a group to be primed and then a 'trial' MLC to be undertaken by each person in the group. The proposal is drafted there and then by each person, but is not individually agreed with the trainer. The MLC is small – three weeks being an optimum time. The group reviews results in a workshop that includes the presentation of new material by the trainer, and the discussion of this. After two or three workshops, and two or three 'trial' MLCs whose subject might be chosen out of curiosity or whim, an individually negotiated contract is established for each person, to run over a two month period.

In this case the 'trial' contracts and the feedback on them provide excellent priming for the managers, who will usually produce clear and effective proposals for the final MLC.

These are all questions the trainer must be able to answer clearly, to reassure the managers that there is a firm structure supporting the relatively free choices they are asked to make (see Box 4.7).

There will also be questions about how certain skills might be assessed – particularly interpersonal skills. An early focus on assessment, however, can lead to MLCs being driven into areas where measures of performance are easier. These will rarely correspond to

---

Box 4.7 A firm structure

Answers to some of the questions as they applied to a development programme run in a large engineering company:

Subject: Anything to do with management of others.
               Discussed and agreed with their own line manager.
               No specifically required forms of self-diagnosis.

Training: MLCs to run over seven weeks.
               Dates specified (giving ten weeks' preparational time, during which other activities would be taking place).

Format: A form was provided which should be filled in and brought to the first meeting as a proposal.

People: Proposal will be agreed and assessed by participant, trainer and line manager.
               At assessment, if any one of these three is not satisfied, the MLC is not complete.

---

actual development needs. The trainer should advise the managers to consider their development needs first, and give assurances that methods of assessment can always be agreed, whatever the area in question

---

Box 4.8 The unquantifiable

Phil was a design engineer by background and had recently become a team leader in an engineering concern. He was well motivated to tackle the development programme, but he appeared shy, precise, more than a little self-conscious, and seemed more than ever uneasy in undertaking the required Management Learning Contract on some aspect of interpersonal skills.

At negotiation and conclusion of the MLC he used the word 'quantifiable' as though it were entirely synonymous with 'assessable'.

His line manager, of a similar background, expressed similar discomfort at making explicit judgements about interpersonal skills and they moved swiftly back to the safety of the world of numbers and analytical skills with results containing decimal points for the next MLC. The main concern of his line manager seemed to be to remove any need for judgement about people from the assessment of the contract.

(Even among design engineers, this is an extreme case.)

Conclusion

The importance of the priming stage can be overlooked only too easily. The Management Learning Contract method is different in significant ways to other, more common, approaches to training or self-development, and it is necessary to introduce it in a manner that respects its difference and its potential.

Diagnosis

In this context, Diagnosis means making an assessment of learning needs, and it leads to decisions about the subject of the contract. Some form of self-diagnosis is recommended, for a number of reasons, the first of which is cost.

Diagnosis by the trainer – an individual training needs analysis – can provide certain advantages: as an outsider, the trainer can take a more objective, dispassionate view of the manager's performance: as an expert (presumed, in some field(s) of management) the trainer can see where things are not working as they should, and can prescribe a remedy. Playing this role of training needs analyst is expensive, however, for the trainer needs to spend time with an individual – observing and discussing, and also learning the singularities of the individual's job – to ensure an accurate as well as an objective and dispassionate diagnosis.

Secondly, we have seen that the motivation of ownership and responsibility is a powerful engine, driving the individual to succeed in tackling a Management Learning Contract. If the trainer diagnoses certain learning needs it is important that the learner/manager genuinely accepts the need for improvement in these areas before an MLC is undertaken. The time taken to gain this genuine acceptance should not be underestimated, and this adds to the cost.

This does not remove training needs analysis from the list of responsibilities fulfilled by the training department. Where any change in technology, policy or legislation creates a new training need for a class of employees or where any shortfall in provision indicates a training need for a group of staff it will be cost effective for the specialists in training to be involved in the analysis.

The increasing popularity of assessment centres as a means of establishing a profile of individual abilities represents an attempt to attain a rigorous analysis of development needs at a reasonable cost, but there remains a trade-off between expense, accuracy of the diagnosis and acceptance of the diagnosis (see Box 4.9).

Box 4.9 Assessing needs

Tom Boydell has set out sixteen different methods of assessing development and training needs, including various types of interview, questionnaires and self-reports, and group discussions (*Boydell 1971*).

The use of Assessment Centres, which feature in the American Management Association work described in Chapter 1, provide a seventeenth possible method.

For the sake of a diagnosis that is acceptable to the individual, congruent with the principles of the Management Learning Contract, and achieved at a reasonable expense, the preferred methods are essentially self-diagnostic.

This may be completely unassisted by the trainer. The manager can simply be primed to prepare a proposal for an MLC, and the derivation of the area for development left to his/her discretion. In some cases this can be very effective: the manager identifies problem areas and brings them to the negotiation. (Indeed, one of the justifications for self-diagnosis is that the individual knows better where problems lie than an outside 'expert'.) In most cases, however, the process benefits from some guidance and support from the trainer.

This can take the form of a structure, or method, which the manager should use in self-diagnosis. There are four common types:

- self-analysis questionnaires.
- obtaining feedback from others.
- using models of good practice.
- selecting from a menu of choices.

Self-analysis questionnaires

This mechanism typically provides a number of statements about activities, feelings or preferences, and the respondent indicates agreement or disagreement. A decoding sheet groups the responses into categories, and aggregates scores for each category. At this point a briefing sheet will make clear the identity of the categories and provide guidance on the meaning of the scores.

A number of general questionnaires, of which the Woodcock and Francis Blockages Questionnaire is probably the best known, aim to deal with the whole range of management activities. There are a large number of specialist examples, dealing with leadership style, teamworking, learning and handling change, time management and so on.

Box 4.10 Know thyself

The **Woodcock and Francis Blockages Questionnaire** uses 110 questions. Responses are decoded into eleven categories, including self-management, problem solving skills, creativity, influence, team-building capacity (*Woodcock and Francis 1975*).

The **Generic Competence Questionnaire** uses the American Management Association model of managerial competence, and asks respondents to rate themselves against the 65 key behaviours (*AMA 1982*).

Of course, any chosen model of competence – a company or industry-wide model, for example – could be adapted to make a questionnaire in this way.

The Management Charter Initiative Competence Standards have been published in a form such that it is possible to use them in this way, but without the decoding and aggregating typical of self-analysis questionnaires: see below under Models of good practice.

Examples of more specialised questionnaires include:

The **Learning Styles Inventory** by Honey and Mumford, where from responses to 80 statements about behaviour a profile of the individual's approach to learning is mapped against the four categories of activist, reflector, theorist, pragmatist. This is very suitable in the context of a training or development programme (*Honey and Mumford 1982*).

A development of this is the **Learning Diagnostive Questionnaire**, which aims to help people match their knowledge and skills, their attitudes and emotions and the learning opportunities available to them at work (*Honey and Mumford 1989*).

The **Management Team Inventory**, by R. Meredith Belbin, enables the respondent to map a personal profile of preferred approaches to team work (*Belbin 1981*).

Other specialised examples are available in abundance, amongst others, in the areas of 'management style' (e.g. *Blake and Mouton 1985*; *Margerison 1979*, delegation (*NRMC 1990*) and time management (*Noon 1985*).

A collection of questionnaires covering a range of areas was published by the Manpower Services Commission (*MSC 1981*).

As an aid to diagnosis prior to undertaking a Management Learning Contract, a general questionnaire can be very useful. A more specialised questionnaire may be appropriate when the manager has already chosen a contract area, prior to the contract being agreed, or even as part of the contract, to establish learning priorities. Alternatively, a range of specialised questionnaires may be used to help managers establish where they stand in a number of key areas.

The use of questionnaires helps the manager towards focus on development through an analysis of personal strengths and weaknesses.

Most questionnaires will show the manager as being strong (scoring well) in some categories and being less strong (scoring badly) in others. The design of the questionnaire sometimes encourages this by creating forced choices between statements. In other cases, where it is technically possible to score the maximum in each category, it is psychologically unlikely.

There are many advantages, therefore, of using self-analysis questionnaires as an aid to diagnosis, but there are also a number of potential drawbacks.

1. *Limited categorisation*: all questionnaires produce results against pre-defined categories. This can lead to a partial, incomplete picture of what an individual's learning needs are or might be.

2. *Accurate categorisation*: it is not always clear, even with sophisticated and well-tried questionnaires, why a certain response to a certain question should indicate, say, a deficiency in a certain category of skills (see Box 4.11). Perhaps this is related in some cases to the following point.

3. *Isolation from the job*: by themselves, the results of the questionnaire are at least one step removed from the manager's real development needs – which are linked to current or future job demands. Development needs indicated by the first results of the questionnaire may be inappropriate in the context of the job, while particular working practices may distort the answers to the questionnaire.

4. *Accurate self-perception:* a major problem with self-analysis questionnaires is the degree to which people are able to assess themselves with accuracy, even if they wish to do so. The simpler tests are vulnerable to motivational distortion, in that an individual may paint a self-image prettier than the life: the more complex tests, which guard against this, need to be decoded by someone else.

5. *Lack of ownership*: finally, the use of a test is the use of a mechanism to which the individual must, to some degree, surrender. After a series of responses to statements of varying relevance, making choices on the basis of inadequate information when in real life the decision would depend upon factors not mentioned in the questionnaire, and deciding between alternatives that appear equally uninteresting, the individual stumbles through an unfamiliar scoring mechanism to find that he/she has serious problems in an essential skill area. It can be easy to disown these results.

Box 4.11 Unclear symptoms

Self-analysis questionnaires often make an association between having a liking for an activity and possessing the necessary skills to do it properly, and the reverse: if I dislike an activity, this is symptomatic of a lack of skill. Preferences of this sort may indeed point to shortfalls in performance, but initially they indicate attitudes: I may like a particular activity because of its relative novelty and because I delude myself as to my level of expertise. I may dislike an activity because I have to do it all the time and I find the exercise of the skill tedious, although I am quite a proficient performer.

Sometimes the jumps between question and diagnosis are greater: one psychometric test gives the respondent the choice between living in a social suburb, or in a deep dark wood, or 'in between'. The sociable suburb and 'in between' count towards an outgoing aspect of personality, and ultimately to a score on the Extraversion scale, although many introverts may enjoy access to society (see *Rowe 1988*).

The potential problems of self-analysis questionnaires in this context can be avoided or minimised by:

- careful choice and thorough exploration of the questionnaire by the trainer prior to use.
- emphasis on the role of the questionnaire as a tool to assist self-diagnosis – not as an arbiter of strengths and weaknesses.
- encouraging managers to consider the results in relation to their job, or to areas for development they had already considered.
- encouraging, where appropriate, managers to discuss results with other people.

Box 4.12 Second opinions

One large company includes in the first stage of its development programme for junior managers a morning when the learner/manager uses the Blockages Questionnaire and his/her line manager also fills in the Questionnaire as if for the learner.

They then spend time together discussing similarities and differences in the profiles they produce, and are encouraged to make some decisions about development priorities.

Managers have included the use of self-analysis questionnaires in their MLC activity on a number of occasions. The most frequent use has been of the Honey and Mumford Learning Styles. The Learner answers on a self-analysis basis: he/she asks others to answer as if for his/her preferences and typical approaches, but the difference can reveal self-delusions or inadequate communication (but see Box 4.14 below).

As a general rule, if a self-analysis questionnaire is a part of the diagnosis system, some time should be made available for managers to discuss the results – with fellow-learners, with their boss or with colleagues – and a trainer should be on hand to answer any queries and to encourage people to see the results in a useful perspective.

Feedback from others

A good means of assessing our strengths and weaknesses is to elicit the opinions of people around us. In the context of MLCs to improve job performance, appropriate people to canvass are our work colleagues and our immediate boss.

If a performance appraisal system operates inside the organisation, the manager will receive some information as a matter of course on areas in which he/she should improve. In other cases, it will be necessary for the learner/manager to take the initiative.

Trainers who propose to use or encourage this aid to self-diagnosis should be aware of the potential barriers. The learner/manager may feel uneasy and unsure how to go about approaching colleagues or the boss, and those approached for feedback may feel equally uneasy and unsure, and may fudge the issue of pointing to weaknesses.

At the same time the potential advantages of accurate feedback economically obtained are considerable. There is much that can be done to smooth progress towards these advantages.

The trainer can:

- provide a format, or a questionnaire, for the manager to give to others. The provision of a format generally helps people structure any feedback. The format can, in addition, include advice or instruction to the respondent to encourage an honest response (see Box 4.13).
- brief the manager on how to approach others, recognising that he/she may find this stressful.
- brief the boss of each learner/manager on the programme, explaining the role of this feedback in the development process, and thereby encouraging honest, positive responses.

It is preferable to treat the feedback obtained as helpful and supportive of the diagnostic task, as information the manager can use in making his/her decision, rather than regarding the manager as being bound by the opinions of others.

It is important to recognise, too, that by creating a system – say through a structured questionnaire – of obtaining accurate, stress-free feedback, we may run the risk of accidentally distorting the results,

Box 4.13 Give it to me straight

Shirley was doing some self-assessment as part of a management course. Did I have five or ten minutes? When we were sitting comfortably she asked if I would tell her what I thought were her strengths and weaknesses as an office administrator. This was rather difficult to do with so little forewarning. Yet she was surprised that a colleague of mine had been unforthcoming under the same circumstances.

A format to encourage a direct and honest response might read like this:

- 'It is difficult to be objective about yourself, or to see yourself as others see you. People can waste a lot of time and energy trying to improve upon what they do in areas where they have no need to improve, and remain unaware of their real development needs.'

- 'Please help me by assessing the questions on the next page honestly and accurately. By doing this you will help me to decide where I should be spending time and effort, and where I should be satisfied with how I am doing right now.'

asking the respondents inappropriate questions, or questions they may not understand (see Box 4.14).

Box 4.14 I can explain

A diagnostic exercise with a number of middle managers from a range of organisations on an open skill development programme used a questionnaire for self-analysis and asked the learner/manager to distribute this same questionnaire to six other people within his/her organisation.

There was a tendency to discount discrepancies in the ratings on the grounds that:

(a) 'That person doesn't see me when I am using that skill.'
(b) 'I don't think they understood the question.'

This was not a universal, or an absolute tendency, but it was reasonably common.

When they were not called upon to comment on every discrepancy, however, the managers did make use of the feedback they had received, focussing on areas of personal concern.

The moral of the experience seems to be that information gained in this way must be treated with caution. Either the majority of decisions about how it will be used should be left with the individual or much carefully directed effort is needed to disentangle the genuine from the phoney reasons for discounting critical feedback.

Models of good practice

Studying a model of good practice can provide the learner/manager with new ideas, benchmarks, points of reference and means of overcoming problems. A realistic model of good practice will encourage personal comparison and the evaluation of one's own performance that is at the heart of self-diagnosis.

The most comprehensive model of good practice in general management in the UK is the competence standards model of the Management Charter Initiative. This sets out the behaviour that might be expected of a competent manager in a number of areas, from matters to do with the provision of a service or product to financial analysis, to leading teams and managing individuals. The model sets out criteria by which we may decide if the manager's behaviour is competent. This model has been produced in a form that makes it relatively easy for managers to use it to assess themselves as a diagnostic exercise. Alternatively, the relevant part of the model can be studied when a manager has chosen a contract area, just as a specialised self-analysis questionnaire might be used, to help shape the details of the MLC (see Box 5.6 in the next chapter).

Most other models of good practice are concerned with particular aspects of manager's behaviour, provide advice about how to achieve results, and advocate certain styles of behaviour (see Box 4.15). This type of model, like the specialised self-analysis questionnaire, is best

---

Box 4.15 A critical model

Kate and Ken Back (1982) set out numerous models of behaviour for difficult situations.

It is not always easy to provide constructive criticism of the work of another person: the outline of the Backs' model for giving criticism breaks it down into seven stages:

1. Check that your inner dialogue is sound.
2. Check that your criticism is specific and not a personal attack.
3. Introduce the topic and, if appropriate, say why you want to raise it.
4. Make your specific criticism.
5. Get a response to your criticism.
6. Ask for suggestions about the desired change.
7. Summarise the suggestions to be actioned.

This is followed by more detailed advice for each stage.

The use of an appropriate model of good practice of this sort in an MLC can provide a firm foundation for making a balanced assessment of personal needs and working towards satisfying them.

employed after the manager has chosen the contract area, either as a precursor to establishing the terms of the contract or as part of the contract itself.

The use of a live role model should not be overlooked in this context.

Box 4.16 A living model

Sarah undertook an MLC on presentation skills, and researched various publications providing advice about the use of visual aids, maintaining eye contact and preparing a clear structure for the presentation, etc. The living example of a sales manager from her own organisation appeared to have more impact on her own style and approach than many of the written principles.

It may be possible for the learner/manager to identify a role model for the skill he/she wishes to develop, and to learn from that person: first by observation, then by reflection on what makes that person a skilled performer. The advantages of a living model are obvious: but it is often difficult to make sense of what one sees. The MLC can help, by focussing the learner's attention on the particular behaviours of the living model that are associated with the skill to be learned.

The menu system

Most training departments will operate a menu system as part of their provision, publishing and publicising the programmes that employees may undertake. When it comes to Management Learning Contracts, providing a list of skill areas from which a learner may choose may seem a good idea: it will open the manager's eyes to the wide range of skills that can be developed, the techniques that can be learned.

The simple menu system is not really a method of diagnosis at all, however, and it can quickly lead to choices being made on the basis of curiosity, novelty or interest rather than development need.

If a menu system is employed for the eye-opening advantages indicated above, the manager should be assisted to ground his/her choice by relating it to job demands and current level of skill, and the menu should indicate MLC areas only, and not provide detailed learning objectives, which might mislead the manager about what he/she really needs to develop.

Combinations

It should be clear that any system which assists self-diagnosis may use a combination of the methods we have surveyed in the last few pages, and the right combination will be the one that best fits local conditions. Whatever system we use, we will be operating within given limits of cost, and accuracy, and the manager's acceptance of the results.

Priming and Diagnosis systems

The Priming and Diagnosis activities which form essential preparation to effective Management Learning Contracts can be brought together in systems that build up the learning momentum of managers undertaking a development programme.

Assistance and guidance in the earlier stages of such a programme appear to be very important. Rather than designing a programme that consists entirely of individualised Management Learning Contracts, it seems more effective to concentrate on some standard, established body of knowledge as a first stage.

This may be no more than a model of competence the company intends to use, and/or a number of different perspectives on the role of a manager, and/or an investigation into a fundamental skill area such as Time Management, which requires some self-examination.

The functions of this are:

- to stimulate thought on the part of the learner and to encourage exploration and self-examination.
- to give the learner time to become used to the idea of preparing an MLC proposal.

If there is a group of learners this also helps to give the individuals in the group time to get to know each other and lay the foundations for any support.

This early period of guided activity may serve to provide both Priming and Diagnostic opportunities, and create a sense of occasion, of general direction and of greater motivation to succeed on the programme.

Summary

In this chapter we have considered how the trainer should help the manager to prepare for an MLC. We have seen that two types of assistance are necessary:

1. Priming which includes

- explaining how MLCs work and why they are being used,
- gaining the confidence of the manager in the MLC approach,
- providing a clear picture of the manager's role.

2. Diagnosis which involves diagnosing or helping the manager diagnose areas of skill in need of development. Diagnosis will always entail finding a balance between

- accuracy,
- cost,
- acceptance of results by the manager.

In the context of using MLCs, the third factor becomes very important and some form of assisted self-diagnosis is preferable.

Priming and Diagnosis activities can be blended together in an introductory stage to any management development programme. This increases the motivation and impetus of the learner/manager.

Exercise

1. Why should an explanation of the Learning Circle be valuable to both Priming and Diagnosis?
2. How can you best gain the confidence of the manager in the MLC method?
3. What are the main drawbacks of self-analysis questionnaires, and how can you overcome them?

Chapter 5

Negotiation

When you have completed this chapter you should be able to:

- **explain the aims and approach of the trainer in negotiating a Management Learning Contract.**
- **distinguish between different types of contract.**
- **identify the different approaches taken by learners/managers to the contract and explain the problems associated with each.**
- **recommend the action a trainer should take when faced with each of the problems.**

Aims of the negotiation

In sitting down to negotiate an MLC with a manager, a trainer's aims should be clear and simple: to agree an MLC that is

- realistic,
- precise and clear,
- owned by the manager.

Sometimes this is a very easy matter, and sometimes unbelievably complicated. By making these three points our focus we are fixing the most important criteria but we are already taking certain things for granted – certain basic rules of Management Learning Contracts that may be supplemented by local constraints or directives.

Realism

Gradual, staged improvement is a key factor in the effectiveness of MLCs. A realistic contract is one that sets the objectives and the assessments at the right level.

Realism of this sort is reached through questions that establish the manager's initial level of knowledge and skill, and then gauge the time and application available against potential learning. A realistic contract in this respect is one that challenges, but does not conquer.

The finer points of levels of achievement are established by the assessment measures, so in that sense realism is an acute assessment problem and we shall return to it in the appropriate chapter.

There is a fundamental enemy of realism, however, against which the trainer must guard from an early stage, and that is the dependency.

Box 5.1 Rules

The rules for MLCs on the Certificate in Management Studies programme at the Northern Regional Management Centre were:

1. The MLC must be about some aspect of management.This is very broad, but rules out the proposals by engineers to iearn more about some aspect of engineering, and librarians to learn more about libraries.

2. It must be a Learning Contract. This, too, is broad, but it is a necessary rule to outlaw the project proposals (see below).

3. It must be a live proposal. It is not a summary, after the event, of learning objectives already achieved. It is establishing a target one hopes to achieve.

4. The initiative in establishing the goal and the objectives of the MLC rests with the programme Participant. The main local rules on the CMS programme were:

5. The MLC is agreed by the Participant, Trainer and a representative of the Participant's employer – usually the line manager – and assessed by them.

6. At least one of the MLCs (out of three) must be about some aspect of interpersonal skills. This is a good rule, requiring some self-examination and preventing a simple chase of techniques or knowledge.

7. The MLC is supposed to take about 40 hours to complete over a six to eight week period.

Dependencies are things the manager is counting on to fulfil the MLC. They come to light in the course of the action plan. They are:

- the manager in the other department who will give some information necessary to completing the contract.
- the training course where the learner will acquire the basic knowledge necessary for the contract.
- the meeting where he/she will practise being assertive.
- the recruitment interview where the interviewing skills will be developed.

And so on (see Box 5.2).

The dependency can only be flushed out by careful questioning. Managers can be unduly optimistic – reckless even – about what will work out for them.

Box 5.2 Dependencies

Eileen saw a major learning opportunity within her own office. A new desk-top publishing system was due to be installed. As office manager, Eileen would need to learn how to use it and then train the remaining office staff. Installation was due the week after this MLC was agreed, and the first tests of the software would begin at once. Eileen would be able to begin learning how to use the equipment within two weeks.

Of course, installation was delayed, the software proved problematic, and the MLC suffered a serious set-back because of this.

Another manager, Colin, aimed to improve his counselling/training skills by working with a supervisor who had difficulties with his self-confidence and with his ability to run Team Briefing meetings. The contract specified that Colin would work with the man for two months, and observe and coach him through four Team Briefing meetings. After the MLC had been under way for a month the supervisor was transferred to another section of the department in an apparently unrelated move.

Louise, a manager in a local authority, aimed to learn how to use Supercalc to calculate the accounts of her section. The local authority offered regular training courses in this and a main resource for her contract was the help and guidance this introductory course would provide. If the courses had run to schedule she could have attended one a fortnight after the contract began. As it was, the course was delayed until after the projected end of her contract.

Another manager, Patricia, had identified a problem in how she dealt with more senior managers in a particular series of meetings, and a contract based on assertiveness techniques, specific to these particular meetings, was agreed. Three weeks after the contract began a re-organisation was carried out and Patricia no longer attended the meetings.

In each of these cases the MLC was delayed or frustrated by an unforeseen change in circumstances, in particular a change to a factor on which the contract was dependent. It is not possible to take account of all of these. In particular, the cases of Colin and Patricia can rarely be foreseen or avoided. The cases of Eileen and Louise, however, are typical examples of dependencies, and similar cases should be thoroughly probed and contingency plans established. This is emphatically the case when dealing with new technology. The machines never arrive on schedule. There are always problems with the software.

Precise and clear

The trainer should ensure that the written agreement accurately reflects what the manager aims to learn and how that learning will be measured, and that the parties to the agreement have a common understanding of what will be done.

With written MLCs of the type used by NRMC, with a Goal Statement, Learning Objectives and Assessment Points, there are levels of gradually increasing precision and clarity. Broad statements are acceptable Goals, but more definition is necessary at Objective level and detailed points are advisable for Assessment.

This is not difficult where the learning area is naturally amenable to clear delineation.

Box 5.3 Precision 1

At first Rob wanted to 'learn something about computers'. After discussion about relevance to his job and his current level of knowledge (minimal) it was agreed that he would learn how to use a Database package in an area of practical use to his job. Specifically, he would produce a Database application that he created, using a standard package, with at least eight fields, and be able to access data through at least four of these, and at least twenty files. He would be able to demonstrate that he could input new data, amend errors to data and access data as requested by the assessor.

Information technology is an area where it is possible to quantify and be precise about targets, and where demonstration of the acquired skills can (and should) be specified in the assessment.

In cases where the manager sets out to improve interpersonal skills, however, precision and understanding may fly out of the window, and it can be helpful – if a little mechanistic – to break these down into knowledge base and skilled action as a method of establishing targets.

As with realism the shoe really pinches when we come to agree on assessment, and we will return to this point in that chapter.

In the meantime let us leave it that a sound approach to take in negotiating the MLC is to go over what has been written, to question and explain, and make sure the same words mean the same things to different people.

Box 5.4 Precision 2

1. Sandra proposed to 'interview three other managers' about management styles as part of her MLC. The inclusion of 'audio-tape equipment for interviews' among the resources indicated that this was intended to be a series of formal affairs. By 'interview' one of her fellow learner/managers had meant 'have an informal chat with'.

2. A common element in an MLC proposal, under 'Assessment' is 'A Written Report'. The trainer who does not seek some clarification of what this will comprise is asking for trouble.

Ownership

It is a fundamental principle of the MLC approach that the learner/manager should own the contract.

Ownership of the MLC gives rise to more commitment to seeing it through, overcoming obstacles and achieving its targets.

Ownership means that the learning area has originated with the manager and that he/she has set out, or participated in setting out, the objectives, the action plan and resources needed, and the performance measures. Throughout the process of establishing the MLC, the manager should initiate proposals, exercise choice between alternatives, accept or reject suggestions from the trainer.

Ownership is a right, and brings with it the power and responsibility to control the MLC. This control operates within certain rules, some of them apparently fundamental to learning contracts, others local to particular training and development programmes (see Box 5.5).

Box 5.5 Owning the contract

General rules on ownership appear to be:

- the learner/manager is required/permitted to take the initiative in devising the MLC.
- the learner/manager chooses the learning area.
- there is some agreement on how and when the MLC will be assessed.
- the agreement is made between a trainer and a learner/manager.

Local rules include:

- constraints may be imposed on the size of the MLC and the length of time it will take to complete.
- the choice of area may be limited to a certain range.
- the format of the assessment may be limited to certain types.
- other parties – e.g. the line manager, other company representatives, colleagues of the learner/manager – may take part in the formation and/or the assessment of the MLC.

If this control is lost, there are two likely culprits: the trainer, and the manager's boss.

The trainer may take control for a number of reasons – through inexperience, because he/she feels more comfortable in a telling, directing role, through frustration with the manager's inability to make a decision or take the initiative.

The manager's boss may take control out of conviction that he/she knows best what the manager needs to develop, or because he/she feels more comfortable in a telling/directing role, or because there is a special, pet project he/she wants the manager to complete.

Both the trainer and the manager's boss have valuable contributions to make to the MLC, but these can be made without the learner/manager losing possession and control of the contract. The responsibility for creating the right environment for this to take place lies with the trainer.

Types of Management Learning Contract

Within the wide variety of MLCs it is possible to see patterns of pure types of contract. In any individual case they may overlap or may, from time to time, emerge in pedigree form. The quality of an MLC is judged on the way it fits the manager, not on its purity of form in this respect, yet it can be helpful to the trainer to recognise the different types.

The Knowledge Contract

The pure Knowledge Contract is one in which the learning objectives are those of acquiring information. The information might be practical and factual (e.g. how the company cost code system works, the correct procedure to follow in routeing products to repair, where I am using my time, what the training needs of my staff are) or more theoretical (e.g. methods of prioritising demands on my time, theories of group behaviour, ideas about origins of stress).

Most skills have a knowledge base, and many well-drafted MLCs will contain a learning objective set in pure knowledge terms. Also the *assessment* of skills contracts can take knowledge as a partial measure. Knowledge has a place.

There is nothing wrong with knowledge contracts, but given the potential scope of the MLC process, it seems that there is not enough right about them, they are too flat and unambitious.

Unless the priming and diagnosis process has been carried out effectively, the manager asked to propose an MLC is likely to suggest a Knowledge Contract, or a project or a Broad Skills Contract. Projects and Broad Skills are treated as problems later in this chapter. We will return briefly to Knowledge Contracts there, too.

The Specific Skills Contract

A Specific Skills Contract looks to define the skill to be developed quite precisely, relating it to a particular feature of the manager's surroundings, e.g. 'improve my ability to understand my company's balance sheet' is a (more) specific skill than 'improve my ability to understand balance sheets'. Similarly 'improve my ability to motivate the fitter operators' is more specific – and may give a more accurate picture of the actual contract – than 'improve my ability to motivate people'.

The competence standards of the MCI model can provide a precise definition of an area of skill, which can be made specific by defining the circumstances in which the competence will be displayed – the particular meeting that will be chaired, the type of information that will be presented.

The Generic Skills Contract

MLCs that deliberately set out to enhance skills which are transferable across a range of situations are Generic Skills Contracts. The ability to

---

Box 5.6 Competence statements

The competence standard of leading meetings is set out below.

Lead meetings and group discussions to solve problems and make decisions

Performance criteria:
- A suitable number of people appropriate to the context and purpose of the meeting are invited and attend.
- The purpose of the meeting is clearly established with other group members at the outset.
- Information and summaries are presented clearly, at an appropriate time.
- Style of leadership helps group members to contribute fully.
- Unhelpful arguments and digressions are effectively discouraged.
- Any decisions taken fall within the group's authority.
- Decisions are recorded accurately and passed on as necessary to the appropriate people. (*NFMED 1990*)

It may be appropriate to agree an MLC such that the learner/manager demonstrates possession of the competence, through actually leading group meetings, on a specified number of occasions.

Alternatively, it may be seen as more appropriate to focus on particular learning areas. The objectives of the MLC might become:

'Improve ability to lead meetings to analyse problems and make decisions, by:
1. improving my ability to identify, encourage and use productive contributions from other members, and,
2. Improving my ability to control digressions from the point of the discussion, and,
3. Improving my ability to recognise and control conflict.'

In this way the MLC picks on sections of the standard that the learner/manager needs to concentrate upon.

be more positive and self-confident, to handle stress more effectively, to be more persuasive are examples of skills that can benefit from a generic approach.

We must be careful to avoid confusing Generic Skills with vague and broad definitions of objectives. It is possible, with a combination of objectives statements and specified performance measures to establish what transferable skills will be developed and how they will be assessed. Generic Skills Contracts can be devised with the help of the model of generic competences of the AMA research or the personal effectiveness model of the MCI.

Box 5.7 Generic competences and MLCs

One of the competences identified by the AMA research is that of Perceptual Objectivity, some of the components of which are:

1. The manager describes another person's point of view on an issue when it differs from his/her point of view.
2. The manager accurately states the differing perspectives that each of the parties in a conflict brings to the situation.

These components could quite easily form the basis of an MLC, as they are clearly stated expressions of competence. Assessment statements would need to specify the type and number of the incidents to be analysed in this way, and establish some means of checking the accuracy of the learner/manager's perceptions: independent testimony is the obvious recourse in this. (*AMA 1982*)

To the extent that there are always limits on transferability, the Generic Skills Contract type moves by degrees towards the Specific Skills Contract type. It is useful to see that, at the poles, there is a clear distinction, without worrying too much at what precise degree one type turns into another.

The Techniques Contract

The pure type of Techniques Contract entails a manager learning a technique he or she has not encountered before, and applying it in practice. Common Techniques Contracts use analytical techniques – Value Analysis, Force Field Analysis, Issue Paper and Ishikawa. In some cases managers have attempted to make progress on large problems by making small, systematic or repetitive changes to their behaviour. The following of these rules in, for example, Time Management (see Box 5.8), or Questioning, is probably best described as a technique.

Box 5.8 Time management techniques

The application of particular rules of behaviour can make a significant difference to the way we manage time. MLC objectives of this nature have included:

- to identify and make use of opportunities for dualling (dualling means doing two things at the same time).
- to use available filters for at least two hours each day I am in the office (filters are methods of stopping or screening interruptions and other calls upon your time).
- to ensure that my desk is empty at the end of each day (this is a performance measure, not an objective).
- to be able to take work home on no more than two nights per week.

$$* \quad * \quad *$$

This last objective was agreed with a manager called Bob, who stuck to it rigorously. At assessment he recalled: 'I was used to taking work home four or five nights a week and at first I didn't know what to do with myself, twiddled my thumbs, watched television. Didn't know what to do with the time.

'I decided I was going to have to do something, so I got involved in voluntary work. The big advantage is, it's something my wife and I can do together. Not like the stuff connected with my job.'

$$* \quad * \quad *$$

Similar approaches to other skill areas would be to pick a particular behaviour or method which is generally a component of the skill and make its fluent practice a contract objective or performance measure.

The Non-Learning Contract

Reaching agreement on what will count as proof that a manager has already attained a certain level of skill or competence is likely to become increasingly common. The purpose of reaching this agreement will be to certificate or to give credit for prior learning or existing ability. Under these circumstances, the objectives of the Non-Learning Contract are likely to be specified and the focus of attention will be on the assessment – that is, the extent to which I as a manager can demonstrate I possess the required skills or competences.

Where the agreement is sought in these circumstances it is entirely legitimate. Where managers are required – for whatever reason – to design and undertake live MLCs the trainer should beware of a natural and human tendency to look for partial or complete ratification of an accomplished statement of intent. It is easier to see what learning has taken place after the event. It is risky to specify targets and performance measures one is not certain of achieving. It is also beneficial, in the most part, to do this and the trainer should ensure that Non-Learning Contracts are agreed only in the circumstances specified above.

Approaching the negotiation

The trainer's best approach to the negotiation is an opening question. After you have shaken hands, made yourselves comfortable and settled in, the trainer should ask: 'What is this contract about?' or 'What do you aim to learn this time?'

As the trainer, you want to set the pattern for the rest of the discussion, and that pattern should be for you to ask questions – mostly short ones – and the manager to provide answers, proposals, statements of intent.

Before you reach this opening question, certain things should have happened:

- the manager should have been primed about his/her role in the MLC process.
- the manager should have had enough time to consider a suitable learning area and objectives.
- the manager should have had some notice of the meeting, to bring the issues fresh to mind
- the manager should know how long the meeting will last.

The same applies to anyone else at the meeting such as the manager's boss. It may be that the latter will need to be briefed at the start of the meeting, but this is bad practice and should be avoided if at all possible. If you, as the trainer, provide this briefing at the beginning of the meeting, it emphasises the control you exercise in policing the rules of engagement, and means you talk too much in the early stages of the meeting.

The general approach should be a questioning one. You want to know what the manager proposes to learn. You may need to be patient and wait while the manager presents the background to the proposal.

The rest of this chapter is about what happens next.

MLC proposals

If all the preliminary and preparatory processes have been carried out properly, the learner/manager should come forward with a clear, realistic proposal for developing his/her management skills. With some minor amendments and clarifications it should be agreed and got under way. Trouble-free MLC negotiations of this sort do take place. There are common problems at the negotiation stage, however, and this section sets out to address them. Managers generally take one of three common approaches to making an MLC proposal.

These can be categorised as the project approach, the skill proposal and the performance problem. Each has its peculiarities, and we shall look at each of them in turn.

The project approach

The project approach is essentially activity-orientated and geared towards producing results in the sense of improvements or changes to working practice, rather than being focussed upon learning, and improvements or changes to personal behaviour. Examples might include: to introduce new technology into a section of the company; to carry out a feasibility study of an operation to compare the advantages of direct against contract labour; to devise a procedure for a new operation; to organise and run a two-day seminar.

It is easy to see why managers may take the project approach.

- they are faced with doing something new and therefore some learning is sure to be involved.
- the project facing them may also be time consuming: incorporating it within an MLC might appear to provide a learning area of a suitable size, and kill two birds with one stone.
- the participant (and his/her line manager) may be more concerned with the short-term benefits of project work (action, leading to results) than the longer term benefit of an MLC (development, leading to improved ability). This may corrupt the negotiation process.
- projects have a longer history as components of management development and training programmes than learning contracts. The priming operation with the participant (and his/her line manager, if this applies) may have failed and there may be genuine misunderstanding about what is required.

It is tempting to class all project approaches by participants as the result of inadequate priming, but where this approach appears for the first reason above – that people are faced with doing something new and therefore some learning is *sure* to be involved – managers may genuinely wish to learn and to develop, and their problem is one of focus and definition.

In essence, however, the primary results-orientation of the project approach interferes with a concern for skill-development.

Problem
Manager concentrates on project, action, results.

Actions
- Establish what they will learn.
- Remind or inform them that the purpose of the MLC is to help them to learn and develop (see 'Priming' in the previous chapter).

Words
'Have you done this type of project before?'
'What is new about it?'
'What will you learn?'
'What you are describing sounds like a project, geared towards producing results in the short term. What will you learn from it? What are you going to focus on for a contract?'

Forms of the project approach
There are two broad sub-species of the project approach. One we may call pure project, the other broad skills collection.

Pure project presents activities as learning objectives.

Box 5.9 The pure project

Mark presented the following proposal as his learning objectives:

1. To produce a manual of services provided by the Manpower Planning Section.
2. To improve understanding, by other departments, of the role of the Manpower Planning Section.

The focus in the first objective is an activity and producing an artefact; in the second case the focus is on the behaviour of others. While the first objective is arguably an example of a highly specific skill it is more plausibly an activity. The underlying knowledge and skills may be the ability to write, structure and present an appealing manual or the ability to relate what the Manpower Planning Section could provide to what the other departments might need.

As anyone who has followed the task, knowledge, skills, attitude format of job analysis knows, there can be initial difficulties in distinguishing between doing something (task) and the ability to do it (skill). This is a particular problem when the social nature of the task means that demonstration of the skill by repeated performance of the task (as in Information Technology skills, or Financial Analysis skills) is not possible.

Problem
Activities are presented as learning objectives.

Actions
- Look to change the emphasis towards development and learning.
- Look for transferable skills within the project.
- Look to establish learning priorities within the actions that are specified.

Words
'These are not learning objectives. I can see what you are going to do – What are you going to learn?'

The broad skills collection typically considers the skills that will be called upon in the course of the project and includes them as learning objectives, defined in broad terms.

Request for further definition will usually lead to additions to this list, still defined in broad terms.

Box 5.10 The broad skills collection

Linda presented the following proposal for an MLC:

'*Goal*
To plan, organise, market and run a training course for [clerical and reception staff within the department] on customer care skills.'
Note that this is a project, not a learning contract, goal.

'*Objectives*
1. Development of training skills.
2. Marketing knowledge and practice.
3. Expansion of planning skills.
4. Knowledge of publicity and advertising.'

The assessment proposals were similarly lacking in detail, and heavily reliant on evaluations carried out by others.

Box 5.10 continued

Of the two groups of skills – training and marketing – it was considered that the training skills would generally be employed and developed the most. The MLC was amended to focus on planning and design skills (assessed through a log and a statement of learning objectives) and actual delivery skills (Linda to identify and describe them, and to receive feedback on her performance).

The marketing element was specified as: an understanding of the market for the course, why this market might attend and how they might be contacted. This omits much of the very broad area of marketing, but it was what was relevant to Linda.

This is not helpful in defining an MLC. The statements are too broad to form objectives or to be assessed. In essence, the problem remains that of a concentration on the project and a lack of attention to or definition of the learning and development aspects of the MLC:

Problem

A number of broad skill areas are proposed as objectives.

Action

Establish development priorities between the skill areas included as objectives and/or define the components of the skill area that will be the focus of the contract.

Words

'I'm sure you're using all of these skills in doing this, but which of them do you really need to develop?'

'We need a better focus to this contract. What marketing skills will you be using to promote this meeting?'

'Which of these areas is most important to you?'

'You have "marketing skills" here. What do you mean by that?'

The process followed is then one quite similar to that of unpacking a Skills Proposal contract.

The skill proposal

Proposals to develop a particular skill or skills are much more in line with the philosophy of the MLC than the Project Approach. Skill proposals come in all shapes, sizes and degrees of detail. Fundamentally they are easier to work with than either of the other two approaches, but they are not without their dangers.

The first, obvious characteristic of the skill proposal is the potential range. Unless the scope is constrained by the training and development programme, a Management Learning Contract should be a broad church, able to accommodate any skill, technique or knowledge that will improve the manager's ability to get things done through other people. These can be strange and wonderful things: from learning pieces of foreign languages, to learning how to use computers to gather, analyse, transform and communicate information; from financial or marketing analyses, to the legion of social and interpersonal skills needed to recruit, motivate, counsel, persuade, lead, discipline, stand up to and get on with other people. Chapter 9 is all about range. The point to be made here is a simple one: it is not always possible to be certain in advance what the focus of the MLC should be. Some managers will present firm and clear proposals – and will produce them in advance if necessary. Others will present more or less clear proposals, but in the course of discussion it will become apparent that the best contract would be elsewhere.

Problem
The manager wants to do a contract in an area you know nothing about, e.g. assertiveness, or neuro-linguistic programming, or cost of capital analysis.

Action
- Try to determine whether the individual really does want to do an MLC in this area (without dissuading them just because you're ignorant: it's meant to be their contract, remember!)
- Find out who does know something about the area – either within the company, among your colleagues, or from an outside agency. Arrange another meeting at which they can be present. Make sure they can take an appropriate part in the assessment.

Words
'Why do you want to do an MLC on neuro-linguistic programming?'
'I'm afraid I don't know enough about neuro-linguistic programming to help you with this.'
'Is there anyone inside the company who could help us with the technical side of this?'

Two longer-term action points: if this happens to you frequently with a particular area you must find some way of dealing with it. Either learn about the area yourself or, if you work as part of a team, establish some form of early warning system so that another member of the team (who is familiar with Neuro-Linguistic Programming) can be present.

Secondly, do not be tempted to claim expertise in an area where your knowledge or skill is weak. If you make suggestions about how skills will be developed you must be prepared for people to take them up, and come back and complain if they didn't work.

In practice, the most common area for trainers to admit their ignorance will be the specific details of the job or the organisation. This can affect their estimate of the realism and the value of the MLC, and also diminishes their ability to assess the results. The role of company expert can best be played by the learner's line manager: some experiences of this are set out below, in Chapter 8.

If the first characteristic of the Skill Proposal is the potential range, the second is the varying degree of detail, from the manager who 'wants to do something on interview skills' to the manager who has broken down a skill area into its component parts, with a means of assessment against each objective (see Box 5.11).

The former, what we have already referred to as the broad skills approach, typically takes a conventional skill area such as making presentations, interviewing, time management, computing. There is less of a tendency to lump together a number of these broad skill areas than in the project approach, because the focus is the skill.

The manager's problem was well expressed by one client of the NRMC, who said: 'It's difficult to set up objectives for a learning contract when you don't know what it is you want to learn.' In this case the manager wanted to 'learn something about computers', but he was looking at the subject from the outside and had difficulty in proposing learning objectives.

Box 5.11 Interviewing skills

Gillian was a junior manager who expected to be involved in recruitment interviewing in the near future. Her learning objectives were:

1. A clear understanding of the procedures to be followed in recruiting a new member of staff to [the organisation].
2. An understanding of the skills necessary to be an effective interviewer.
3. Recognition of my own strengths and weaknesses in using these skills, and
4. Development (through practice) against priority areas of weakness.

Problem
Manager proposes a broad skill area.

Action
Establish what the manager means by the expression, and whether he/she can be more precise about the learning objective.

Words
'So you want to improve your marketing skills. What do you mean by "marketing skills"?'
'What kind of interviewing skills do you mean? Appraisal, counselling, recruitment?'

It may be that this line of questioning will reveal that the manager has a very clear idea of what he/she wants to achieve, in which case all is well. It will also reveal some managers for whom the skill area is a black box – whether it be computing, marketing or counselling.

Problem
Manager has very little knowledge base for the skill area.

Action
The trainer has a choice here, between trying to establish through questioning the most relevant aspect of the skill area to the manager or, alternatively, suggesting objectives that lead the manager to acquire a knowledge base across the whole area. Let's call these Plan A and Plan B.

Words
Plan A:
'What kind of information do you want to put on the computer?'
'Which part of this is new to you?'
'Which is the most important part of this to your job?'
'What do you want to be able to say in Dutch?'

Plan A scripts may also involve giving some brief description of the possibilities and asking the manager for indications of preference.

Plan B:
'Perhaps the first thing is to have a clear idea of what the area involves. The three most common computing programmes are Spreadsheets, Databases and Wordprocessing. Suppose we say you'll be able to explain what each of them can do as your first objective?' (Note: you should have established that the manager doesn't already know this.)

This approach involves directing the manager. There are two necessary implications.

1. The trainer is becoming more of a leader, a teller, an owner of the contract and the manager is becoming more of a follower, a person who is told, and less of an owner of the contract. It is important to suggest rather than to direct, and to look to give the manager choices.
2. The trainer needs to know enough about the area to specify the parameters of the knowledge base. If not then a specialist needs to be brought in to the discussion.

The model for this approach to an MLC is:

- acquire knowledge of good practice.
- compare own performance with good practice and establish learning priorities.
- concentrate on a limited number of learning priorities, and look to make progress against them over a fixed period of time.
- evaluate progress and consider an action plan for further development.

The broad skills proposal is typically brief and can be spotted quite quickly with a little experience.

The detailed Skills Proposal is typically wordier and evidently the product of thought and effort. If it proves to be problem free, it is the only type of proposal likely to be agreed and signed without amendment.

Potential problems
- The wording of the objectives, activities or assessment points is ambiguous, leading to different perceptions of the MLC.
- The proposal is unrealistic, involving more time and effort than is practicable, or access to information or resources that will not be available.

Action
Check out both of the above points by talking through each part of the proposal with the manager.

There is one further potential problem to consider in handling a Skills Proposal: the proposal may be the manager's solution to a perfomance problem and it may be the wrong solution (see Box 5.12).

An apparently sensible MLC could be agreed that would result in no skill development (because lack of skill is not the cause of the performance problem) or disenchantment (because the skill development does not result in the resolution of the problem).

Box 5.12 The wrong solution

Mike wanted to improve his performance in meetings. Recently he had been embarrassed on more than one occasion in meetings with clients. He presented his contract as one which focussed on better preparation for these meetings, and an improvement in his abilities to make formal presentations to customers.

Fortunately discussion with his line manager before the MLC began cast doubt on the benefit of these measures. It was indicated that some specific aspects of presentation skills could be improved upon, but that another dimension of the problem concerned self-confidence in discussing matters with customers and more senior managers. It was decided to focus the MLC on Mike's feelings, through a logging process, and on developing 'scripts' to handle situations he found difficult – which meant changing some of the sentence structures he commonly used.

Preparation and formal presentation skills did not appear in the MLC. They were low priority – or no priority – learning areas.

It is good practice, therefore, to ask why the manager wants to undertake development of the chosen skill and, if appropriate, to question the diagnosis that points to this skill area as the solution to that problem.

The performance problem

In approaching the agreement of an MLC from the Performance Problem viewpoint, managers are typically concerned with a difficulty, a problem or an aggravation, but they are not sure what to do about it. They outline the problem and look to the trainer for advice, with greater or lesser expectations of a miracle cure. Examples include the manager who wanted to get more commitment from his team, the manager who wanted to have more impact in meetings, the manager who has suffered from stress or from time pressure problems, the manager who wanted to gain more respect from his colleagues and more credit for the ideas he produced.

In some cases, the approach taken by the learner/manager will fall somewhere between the Skills Proposal and the Performance Problem. We have seen that some Skills Proposals are the result of diagnosing performance problems, and suggested that the reason for Skills Proposals be probed. In some cases the initial explanation by the manager will be of the performance problem, followed by the Skills Proposal. This is more common when a skill area appears easily applicable – e.g. time management problems are solved with time management skills, and stress management problems are solved by learning 'something about stress management'. Of course it is not as simple as this, even in those areas where a limited number of techniques exist and there are clusters of core ideas.

In the areas of managing or relating to other people the actual skills and the means of developing them may be much more difficult to define.

In some cases this is because the problem has not been well defined, or the causes of the problem have not been identified. The first steps to take with the manager who wants to have more impact in meetings, for example, involve finding out what this means. What meetings? What does he/she want to achieve? How are people reacting to him/her now? How does he/she want them to react?

Sometimes the problem can be accurately identified before the contract is agreed, and its causes narrowed down to a limited range of possibilities. In most performance problem MLCs a part of the contract entails analysing the problem and the learning priorities.

In these cases the model of the learning contract is:

- gather and record information on the problem: when it occurs, what are the symptoms, what are the possible causes?
- identify priorities in tackling the problem.
- identify techniques or best practices to handle priority areas.
- apply techniques over a period of time, and evaluate progress.
- specify an action plan for further development (see Box 5.13).

Establishing possible causes of the problem may entail an excursion into theory, or acquiring facts or information from colleagues (see Box 5.14).

The manager is likely to look to the trainer for suggestions as to further reading, or as to constructs or methods for gathering and analysing information from others. The proposal that the problem should be tackled using the model outlined above will almost certainly need to come from the trainer.

The subordinate's problem

At NRMC we have been approached on a number of occasions and asked by a senior manager to help a more junior manager who 'has a problem'. In a similar vein, it is sometimes evident in MLC negotiations that the impetus for focussing on a performance problem area comes not from the learner/manager but from his/her boss. Can MLCs work under these circumstances?

Box 5.13 Performance problem contract

Mike's MLC (see Box 5.12) was:

Goal
To develop techniques to improve my ability to feel more comfortable and to deal more professionally and confidently with more senior managers and customers.

Objectives
1. To identify occasions in dealing with other people, particularly senior managers or customers, when I feel comfortable and in control, and occasions when I don't.
2. To have a clear understanding of what I am already doing right and what I could do better in those situations.
3. To improve my ability to handle situations where I currently feel uncomfortable.
4. To understand how to develop further.

Assessment
1. Analyses of at least six occasions, setting out what happened, what I did right, what I could do better next time, how I felt.
2. Brief written statement and oral explanation of conclusions about what I could do.
3. Review of progress of attempts to use different methods of handling the situations.
4. Brief written statement and oral explanation of remaining immediate barriers.
5. Statement of action plan for further progress.

Activities
1. To identify techniques, from reading, that I think I could use.
2. To identify other people who handle 'difficult' situations well and to analyse how they say things and how they respond to pressure.
3. To analyse situations where I deal with seniors and customers; considering points set out in Assessment 1.

This pressure from a more senior manager can seriously threaten the ownership and control of the MLC, which should reside, as we have said, with the learner. The MLC will only be effective if the learner:

- accepts there is a problem.
- believes something can be done about it.
- is prepared to do something about it.

If any of these three conditions does not apply, learning is very unlikely to take place (see Box 5.15).

Box 5.14 Sources of information

A supervisor in a busy factory run on a team system was concerned that his ability to represent his point of view in meetings was letting him down.

A contract was agreed whereby he would:

- arrive at a clear picture of the skills required to contribute to meetings – this from reading practical texts and observing colleagues, and then making his own list.
- establish his strengths and weaknesses in terms of these skills – this he did by using a scoring system for himself, and also asking his immediate boss to score him.

In this way, he drew on the published ideas of others, and the perceptions of someone close to him.

Other learner/managers have given questionnaires to colleagues – such as the Honey and Mumford Learning Styles Questionnaire – and asked for feedback on their behaviour in this way.

Box 5.15 The imposed contract

At the first of the three discussions to establish Vic's Management Learning Contracts for the CMS programme it was evident that there were differences of opinion between Vic and his boss. Alan, the Project Manager, found Vic disorganised, haphazard, badly prepared, and suggested Vic should do a time management contract.

Vic rejected this strenuously, and got agreement that his first MLC would be on another area.

Throughout his period of involvement with the programme there were external difficulties – re-organisation of his section, with enforced redundancies always a possibility, and wide fluctuations in the workload. It was also apparent that he was a poorly organised individual who overshot deadlines and failed to keep appointments. This realisation was always resisted by Vic, who would point to all manner of reasons outside his control why he had not met his targets. Eventually he failed the programme: he ran out of time.

Generally the imposed contract requires the employer's representative to bring the problem to the learner/manager's attention and *gain agreement that it is a problem*. If this is not done, the MLC will not work as a means of correcting the problem. A more effective path will probably be disciplinary action for the performance failures.

The presentation of a Performance Problem as subject for an MLC can be a genuine and productive approach. It may not be so neatly packaged as a Skills Proposal, but the effects may be more significant, useful and durable.

The knowledge proposal

Earlier in this chapter we encountered the MLC that had as its objectives the acquisition of knowledge, whether factual information or theory. We meet it again here as a problem child, a contract that is barely respectable given the scope of the MLC for skills development. Without careful priming and manager understanding the knowledge contract proposal is very common because:

- it is easy to define information that one would like to know, or can learn, but it is more difficult to define skills.
- it can be more acceptable to admit to not knowing information in a certain area, whereas it may be less acceptable (or more risky) to admit to skills needs.
- a knowledge contract is the easiest translation of a project into a contract.

Box 5.16 From project to knowledge contract

Brian's pet project, which he presented as a contract proposal, was to research and produce a manual setting out the systems and procedures for people in his division of a large department to use when dealing with people from other divisions. His division, heating maintenance, serviced other divisions on request, and in some cases required the co-operation of other divisions – for example, building services – to complete their work.

When it was put to him that this was a project and not a learning contract, and he was asked what he would learn from this, the predictable reply was:

'A better understanding of the systems and procedures governing the relationship between heating maintenance and other divisions within the department.'

In other words, a straightforward knowledge contract.

As Brian already knew a great deal about these systems and procedures, it was difficult to see whether the MLC would be at all valid.

The measure that may be taken is simply to outlaw knowledge contracts and to insist that all MLCs on your training and development programme are focussed on skills. Failing that, you should negotiate.

Problem

Manager produces an MLC proposal that aims to 'find out about' or to 'understand' facts, procedures or processes in the organisation, market or environment.

Action

- Look to make explicit other stages of the Learning Circle. If the original proposal is about Knowledge, it may be possible to move part of the contract towards the preparation of an action plan, in the light of the new knowledge. This amendment can be made to the objectives and to the assessment points.

This, at least, involves the use of analytical skills, if not their development.

- Alternatively, look to move the focus partly towards how this information was gathered. This is particularly appropriate for the process of gathering of factual information from others. Again, this can be suggested as an inclusion to objectives and assessment points.

Words

'I think there's an important part of this contract missing from the proposal. It's something you're going to do that isn't set down here yet'.
'Let's take this just one stage further.'

Levels of preparation

We have already seen some examples of the different degrees to which learner/managers prepare for discussions on the MLC, from the identification of a broad learning area (Time Management, Interviewing Skills, etc.) to a detailed proposal based on thoughtful analysis. As a final stage in our examination of approaches to the MLC, let us consider some of the problems arising from these levels of preparation.

No proposal

Priming and diagnosis may have failed, and the manager arrives at the negotiation with no proposal to make. This tends to indicate lack of commitment or organisation.

The trainer's options are:

- to attempt to establish, from this cold start, a development need the manager might address and draw up an MLC. This is hard work and is unlikely to produce an MLC to which the manager feels committed.
- to discuss how the manager might carry out some diagnosis of his/her needs and arrange to discuss the MLC at a later date.

- to re-state the priming requirements, that the manager makes a proposal, and cut the discussion short.

The choice between alternatives

Sometimes the manager will present a choice between a number of different MLCs. Particularly if this is the first contract the manager and trainer have met to discuss, the manager might express some uncertainty about whether MLCs in a particular area are acceptable

If all of the options are acceptable it is advisable for the trainer to push the choice back to the manager, to emphasise where the responsibility lies. The major problem of encountering the Choice Approach is then the unanticipated and unscheduled length of the discussion which ensues as the manager talks through the range of alternatives.

The detailed draft

A detailed draft MLC proposal indicates enthusiasm and commitment. Problems can arise, however, if the effort has been misguided – such as when a Broad Skills Collection is presented. A good general rule, to leave ownership with the manager and to avoid dismotivation, is to make the minimum number of amendments necessary. The Broad Skills Collection will need radical surgery, but Specific or Generic Skills Proposals may only suffer from a little imprecision or a shade too much (or too little) ambition.

In the case of minor amendments, best practice is to focus on clarifying the Assessment Points – usually to make them more specific. While other aspects of the MLC may be less than ideal in a technical sense it is better to let them pass and retain the learner's motivation, as long as the assessment is precise and realistic.

Summary

In this chapter we have considered the negotiation and agreement of MLCs. We have established the trainer's aims in entering the discussion, that the MLC is:

- realistic
- precise and clear
- owned by the learner/manager
- and we have seen how these aims must sometimes be traded off against one another.

In negotiating MLCs the trainer will encounter a wide range of learning areas and methods. It is well to bear in mind the different pure types of MLC:

- The Knowledge Contract
- The Techniques Contract
- The Specific Skills Contract
- The Generic Skills Contract
- The Competence Contract

It should be remembered that these may overlap in any particular set of circumstances.

Finally, the trainer will meet with different approaches to the discussion from learners/managers, each with its different problems. The common approaches are:

- The Project Approach
- The Skills Proposal
- The Performance Problem
- The Knowledge Proposal

Each of them challenge the trainer in different ways.

Exercise

1. Why do the objectives of agreeing a realistic and precise MLC sometimes conflict with the objective of having the manager retain ownership of the contract?
2. What are the four pure types of MLC?
3. What are the problems inherent in the Project Approach? What might be the cause of a number of Project Proposals from a group of managers?
4. What is the model of an MLC to deal with a Performance Problem?

Chapter 6

Assessment

When you have completed this chapter you should be able to:

- describe the different types of evidence that can be used to assess a Management Learning Contract.
- suggest appropriate methods of assessing different MLCs.
- explain how you would establish criteria for assessing an MLC.
- set out the aims of a trainer in carrying out an assessment, and describe how these aims may be achieved.

The importance of assessment:

In discussing Management Learning Contracts to this point, we have distinguished between learning objectives and assessment measures. Learning objectives make some specification of what is to be learned, while assessment measures give a more precise statement of what will be produced or demonstrated to prove that the learning objective has been achieved. In this sense the assessment measures act as more precise targets than the learning objectives themselves.

Box 6.1 Learning objectives and assessment measures

Examples might include:

Learning objective
Have an understanding of how I am using my time and how this relates to the priorities of the job.

Assessment
A log of how I have spent my time on work or work-related matters for a two-week period, with each activity analysed as to priority, using the ABCX system of priorities.

Learning objective
Be more assertive in refusing unreasonable requests for assistance from managers in other departments.

Assessment
An account of at least four occasions when I have refused unreasonable requests from other managers:

Box 6.1 continued

- an assessment of my behaviour as to how
  - honest, firm and direct
  - problem-centred
  - confident

it was

- an assessment of my feelings as to whether I felt:
  - under pressure
  - guilty
  - angry
  - calm
  - confident

There are different views on the importance of assessment to the use of MLCs. On the one hand it is held to be fundamental to the whole process.

- Assessing progress against the agreed measures is a means of evaluating whether the MLC is effective or not.
- The precision of the targets enhances the learner's motivation.
- The involvement of another person in assessing the MLC at a specified time enhances motivation and the accuracy of the evaluation.
- Assessment is necessary if any kind of certification or recognition is to follow successful completion of the MLC.

There is another view, however, which recognises the merit of assessment, but argues that an action planning or contracting approach can be of value to the individual without necessarily involving assessment by another person (*Powers 1987*).

Certainly the processes of self-diagnosis, of planning specific steps to enhance knowledge or skill, and of setting personal targets against which to measure oneself, can be of great value in self-development. The disadvantage of assessment by some other person for some other purpose may be that the original goal of personal development for its own sake becomes subverted into the achievement of the performance measures for the sake of extrinsic reward. The effort which could otherwise go solely towards self-development can be divided between the linked goals of (a) developing self and (b) proving that development has taken place.

Sometimes the division favours the latter, unproductive goal at the expense of the former. Equally, there is a danger in evaluating training programmes according to the enjoyment, satisfaction or professed illumination they provide the participants. Training should be about development and enhanced performance, not entertainment. So despite the risks inherent in the attempt, the advantages of assessment are generally worth while.

The remainder of this chapter is about establishing a realistic assessment of the learner's progress.

Measuring success

There is a wide range of methods for assessing improved performance, each one with its strengths, each with its drawbacks. The project report or written assignment, so long beloved of colleges and validating bodies, has the value of being recorded, tangible evidence, expedient to administer and assess, with the potential drawbacks of being only loosely connected to developments of skill and demanding much displaced effort on the part of the writer. There are, of course, alternatives to the conventional written report, which assess development more accurately and which make fewer unproductive demands on the learner's time and effort.

For each MLC there are ideal methods of assessment, and also limitations on the ideal. Some limitations are simply due to the unco-operative, sometimes intractable nature of reality, other constraints relate to the vagaries of the particular self-development scheme (particularly if success leads to certification or some other form of recognition) which may determine who carries out the assessing and the form the assessment must take. The level of available resources (number of assessors, time available, audio-visual equipment, etc.) will also limit what can be done.

Working within these limits it is possible to move closer towards the ideal with the Management Learning Contract approach than with any other method of development. This is because the assessment measures are agreed as part of the contract, and so should be as snug a fit as the law, the budget and awkward reality will allow.

Designing assessment

Two aspects of assessment immediately strike the parties to a Management Learning Contract. How can a particular skill be assessed – that is, what kind of evidence is required? Secondly, what standards must that evidence meet?

Box 6.2 Evidence and criteria

Managers generally have little difficulty in suggesting forms of evidence – although the forms they suggest are perhaps not always the most appropriate. Generally, they have difficulty in suggesting criteria, and may swing from the extreme of quantifying increased output to the other extreme of relying on the judgement of the trainer or specialist.

To define criteria is to do no more than to define certain properties of the evidence. I may seek to prove my skills as a trainer have improved by, among other things, producing feedback questionnaires from people who have attended sessions I have led during the course of my contract. This is a *form of evidence.* We then might consider criteria: we should specify how many sessions, how many questionnaires: perhaps we would specify what the questionaires should cover – or require me to provide a reasonable justification of what I have included: perhaps we should specify an improvement will be shown in one or more areas or that a reasonable explanation can be given as to why any improvements are not reflected in the questionnaires.

The danger of using the questionnaires as the sole means of assessing improvements should be obvious to any trainer!

We have not eliminated judgement by any means; what comprises a reasonable explanation or a reasonable justification is a matter of judgement. We have defined the areas in which judgement will operate.

We could go further (particularly with 'reasonable justification') and define clearer and more detailed criteria. Whether we do so may depend on the time available to us to agree the MLC, and the extent to which this might threaten the manager's sense of ownership of the proposal.

The answers to both these questions should be set out clearly in the MLC document

Which takes us to the third aspect of assessment, less immediately obvious to the parties to the contract: Who designs the assessment? Let us deal with this issue first.

Who designs the assessment?

The short answer to this question is: The assessment measures, like the rest of the MLC, are agreed by all the parties to the contract. In that sense the design of assessment measures is a joint venture.

This is true, so far as it goes. But while the trainer is advised to stay well clear of proposing new learning objectives (see Chapter 5) it may be appropriate for the trainer to take more initiatives here, including proposing new measures of assessment.

There are four good reasons why this should be so:

1. The success of the MLC will depend on the achievement of targets proposed in assessment, so these must be more precise than any other part of the MLC. The need to change the original proposal is more likely to arise in this section of the contract than any other.

   This comes about partly as a result of . . .

2. Managers seem to have more difficulty preparing assessment measures than designing any other area of the MLC. They will often put forward inappropriate or vague suggestions.

   The trainer will have a better grasp of the principles of learning and assessment than most managers in this position, and will be able to make suggestions that are recognised as logical and reasonable.

3. The sense of ownership, which is important to success of the MLC method, should already have been established if the manager has chosen the learning area and proposed learning objectives and a plan of action which have been accepted with no more than minor amendments. Proposals to change the assessment measures, if they are reasonably discussed and agreed, should not seriously threaten that proprietorial feeling.

4. Where a number of managers are undertaking MLCs as part of a development programme, the trainer who is involved in several contracts may legitimately suggest a raising or lowering of standards – involving additions or subtractions in the assessment area – in the name of parity between participants.

Of course, like the rest of the MLC, the assessment measures should be agreed by all the parties to the contract, and not imposed by the trainer.

The trainer's role here is to clarify the vague points of the manager's proposal, to suggest that some proposed assessment measures are unnecessary, to put forward replacements or additions, and to be able to explain the reasons for each of these actions.

What kind of evidence

How can I prove that I have developed a particular skill? It may be difficult enough proving it to myself – but how do I prove to you, my trainer, friend or colleague, that I have developed this skill?

The easiest way might be to show you, arrange a demonstration. Sit me before a computer terminal and I will use a spreadsheet, add to it, draw from it, amend its shape. Bring me a balance sheet and I will demonstrate my ability to read and analyse it. And so on.

But what if the skill is not amenable to demonstration, on demand? Like handling grievances, it might be a skill that is only demonstrated behind closed doors or, like time management or team leading, it may be seen only in hundreds of small actions over reasonably long periods of time.

In some cases, we might set up a situation, a simulation, where I can demonstrate the skill. In other cases you might have to believe my account of what I have done. Perhaps the testimony of other witnesses would help to convince you. Perhaps the results of my skilled behaviour, measured in cost or productivity terms.

In picking a path through the options of types of evidence, it is good to bear in mind the principles of skill development on which the MLC process is based.

You will remember from Chapter 3 that a learner develops a skill by going through a series of stages, set out as stations on the Learning Circle.

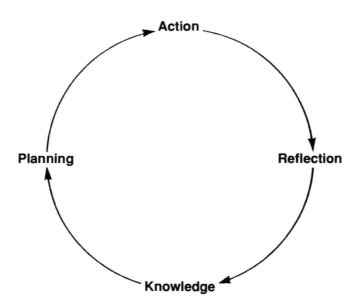

Figure 6.1 The Learning Circle

If the action (the demonstration of skilled behaviour) is not available for assessment, then other stages of the Learning Circle may be used as surrogates. Even if the action is available for inspection, you should also explore some of the other situations, to ensure the action is deliberate (planning), to ensure it is understood (reflection and knowledge).

With this principle firmly in mind, let us consider the following types of evidence:

- Demonstration
- Simulation
- Tape-recording
- Witness Testimony
- Personal Report
- Products and outcomes.

Demonstration

The learner/manager demonstrates to the assessor that he/she can perform the actions that make up the skill. This may usefully be accompanied by some discussion and explanation.

Demonstration is particularly appropriate for contracts where the manager has undertaken to learn some aspect of computing (see Box 6.3).

Box 6.3 The Black Box

The manager who is exploring information technology for the first time by means of an MLC is ill-equipped to suggest assessment measures, and this is a clear case of the initiative naturally coming from the trainer. Assessment measures for an MLC that sees a manager taking the first steps in using a database might be:

1. Production of a database constructed on a standard package: to contain data relevant to my job, and to contain at least 20 files and eight fields. Access to the data will be through at least three fields.
2. Demonstration of ability to use the database by accessing the data, adding a new file, correcting a detail in a file.
3. Oral explanation of how database programmes could be used in other areas of my job (if applicable).
4. Oral report on any barriers, problems or difficulties I encountered in tackling the contract, and how I overcame them.

This last point is to encourage the manager to reflect explicitly upon his/her experiences, with an emphasis on successful achievement. It may help the learner to make realistic plans for further development in understanding and using computers and/or in designing any future Management Learning Contracts.

The Action part of the Learning Circle can be observed directly in these cases. Similarly, when a manager has undertaken to improve his/her ability to understand a set of financial accounts, the best means of showing that improved understanding may be by means of a demonstration – in this case a presentation, with questions. If a manager has undertaken to improve upon the use of an analytical technique in a general sense (i.e. so that he/she can use it in a wide range of circumstances) it may be appropriate to assess the improvement by demonstration.

Demonstration is generally not practical in the interpersonal skill areas – although there may be some exceptions, such as presentation skills, where the assessor can be part of the audience (see Box 6.4). Generally, however, it is not possible for an assessor to sit in on a meeting where the learner/manager demonstrates improved skills in conducting a disciplinary interview, or in counselling an employee about a personal problem, or in negotiating about resources with representatives of other departments, and so on. In some cases confidentiality is the issue: an outsider – an assessor or a trainer – will not be given access to the forum for the display of skill. In some cases the assessor can be present, but his/her presence would disturb the normal course of events so much that the demonstration assumes the unreality of a simulation. In some cases the occasion on which the skill will be displayed is so unpredictable, or takes place over such a long period of time, that it is impracticable for an assessor to witness a demonstration (being assertive in handling put-downs might be an example of the former, time management an example of the latter).

Box 6.4 Just pretend I'm not here

There are degrees of unreality even in presentation skills MLC assessments.

In one case, John, an engineering manager in a large corporation, was able to use a formal presentation he was scheduled to deliver, to an audience of 150 people, as part of his assessment. The trainer and John's boss were able to find inconspicuous seats at the back of the auditorium and view the performance from there.

In another case, Jennifer, who worked for the publications section of an engineering company, used a presentation to ten representatives of other departments for her presentation. The trainer was an obvious outsider and the audience was aware that whilst the presentation was serious, there was a dual purpose to the occasion.

Finally, Matthew proposed an oral presentation on the computerised work-flow system within his department. The trainer on this occasion made up 25 per cent of the audience, and the circumstances for a fair and realistic assessment of Matthew's skills were far from ideal.

Simulation

Assessing skills through assessing behaviour in simulations of one sort or another has a long history in all kinds of training. Where the actual Action is inaccessible – perhaps, as above, for reasons of confidentiality – it is a temptation to establish a set of circumstances that *should* test the same skills. With the Management Learning Contract method, this is most likely to suggest itself in the interpersonal skills area. It is not possible for the assessor to sit in on, say, an actual recruitment interview – so why not set up a mock interview, which can be observed and assessed?

The major problem with assessing skills through simulation is the issue of transferability: is it true that skills developed and assessed in classroom situations can actually be applied directly to real life circumstances? Is it sufficiently true that the assessment of skill in a simulated situation can be taken for the presence of skill in a real situation?

This is an issue on which there are opposing views. The effectiveness of the simulation as an assessment vehicle must depend upon:

- the extent to which it resembles actual circumstances in which the manager will use the skills to be assessed, or
- the extent to which it is a fair test of generic skills or techniques the manager has undertaken to develop.

The distinction between specific and generic skills is a crucial one. It is one thing to develop generic skills of, say, recruitment and selection, and another to develop skills of recruitment and selection for my own department inside my particular company (see Box 6.5). If the generic skills contract is undertaken, a simulation interview might form part of the assessment, but one would also expect questions that would test me on the differences between any of the assessment procedures and the actual reality existing inside my company.

Box 6.5 Skills and procedures

In most large organisations there are rules and procedures governing how to go about recruitment and selection, and some of the specific skills appropriate to that organisation concern being able to apply the rules and operate the procedures. Even the core skills – of job analysis, job specification, employee specification and interviewing – may be so strongly flavoured by the organisation's culture that it is only when the common practice is patently bad practice that the manager can see any value in exploring alternative, better ways of behaving.

Action in a set of circumstances designed to simulate reality can be considered as a form of evidence, but proposals to use this form of assessment should be treated with caution.

Tape recordings

The Video Tape Recording (VTR) is a frequent companion to the simulation, particularly for set pieces such as interviews, presentations or meetings. The training resources available within the company will dictate whether or not it is a possible option. Other circumstances will indicate whether it is also a wise option.

Much of what has been said about simulations in assessment can be read again in application to the use of VTRs.

In addition, we might note:

- video equipment often lends a further air of unreality to a simulation. Lights, sound recordings, the position of the chairs, the extra apprehension of a manager, if he/she has not seen himself on film before.
- video distorts some aspects of behaviour, making hesitations, ums and ahs and some aspects of body language appear much more significant than they are in reality.
- video does enable a manager to comment critically on his/her performance after the event. (What is said and omitted in this commentary often gives a better indication of the manager's awareness of what is entailed in the skill than the tape itself.)
- video enables repeated viewing and detailed constructive criticism from an assessor or a trainer, which the manager can use in conjunction with the tape.
- the danger of assessing what is on the video tape *because it is easy to assess*, should be guarded against if the aim of the MLC is to improve the exercise of a skill in the workplace.

Simulations and VTR can be of great value in developing skills, but both should be approached with great caution when it is time for assessment (see Box 6.6).

Audio tape is becoming a neglected medium in many training departments. Less obtrusive than a video recording, it may be of value in capturing a record of real action, where video would be impossible but the assent of other parties may be given to taping the meeting, or the interview. This will never be more than a partial record of action, of course, but it can provide a piece of evidence on which questions and further explanations can be hung (see Box 6.7).

Box 6.6 Lights, action . . .

Neil undertook an MLC on selection interviewing skills, and he proposed a videotape of a simulation as the main means of assessment. After some discussion it was agreed that the evidence for assessment would include the job specification and an explanation of Neil's plan as to how he would assess the 'applicant' against the specification. An evaluation by Neil of his own performance (it was suggested that he make an evaluation before viewing the tape, and then see what the tape added, but this suggestion was not incorporated as a term in the MLC) would be accompanied by a statement of the skills Neil thought were important to good interviewing, and an estimate of his own strengths and weaknesses.

Oh, yes, and the tape itself, of course.

Where Neil had proposed simply a record of the action, the final assessment took in planning, reflection and evaluation, too.

Box 6.7 I will say this only once

Audiotape is particularly useful for assessing skills in speaking a foreign language, particularly if the logistics of bringing the manager face to face with a fluent speaker of the particular language are tricky. A tape, with an accompanying translation – in transcript or tape format – can be sent to a specialist for assessment. (Obviously it is important to be quite clear in setting out the criteria for success, so that the specialist may use them for guidance).

Testimony of witnesses

The testimony of others can be a helpful element in assessment of a contract. This is so particularly when:

- the other person will be a natural witness to the exercise of the skill that is targeted by the MLC (see Box 6.8). Where it would be impossible or inconvenient for the assessor to be present, or the other person is an expert witness, by virtue of his/her special knowledge: the most frequent occurrence of this is likely to be when this is local knowledge of the organisation, its procedures and priorities, but it may also be specialist professional knowledge – of say, accounting or project management or operational techniques – that needs to be brought to bear.

Box 6.8 The recruitment panel

Carol's second MLC was to develop her recruitment interviewing skills. Most of the assessment was based on a personal report of what she had done (some reading, five live interviews, some reflection and analysis). Her boss was present during three of the interviews and he was able to corroborate certain aspects of her account.

Box 6.9 The expert and the local witnesses

When managers use the detail of their real work environment as part of their MLC, it can create a difficulty for the trainer. The planning report looks well structured, but its contents are beyond the trainer's technical knowledge: the manager sets out the priorities he believes the Department should apply – and the trainer has little idea of whether or not these are realistic: another manager brings along the proof that she can use Force Field Analysis – a report on the factors that influenced a particular committee on a recent decision – and the trainer needs someone who can verify the facts.

In these cases the trainer can test the logical consistency of the manager's viewpoint, and by raising questions of detail may be able to assess some dimensions of credibility or depth of understanding, but it is necessary to be able to turn to someone who has real knowledge (usually the manager's boss) or expert knowledge (the company finance manager, export manager, systems analyst, etc.) and ask for confirmation of the accuracy of the facts. Learners/managers will almost always accept and respect this.

Among the Natural Witness category can be accounted those cases where a number of people provide information on performance, the most frequent example being the completion of evaluation forms by people who have formed the audience of a learner/manager working to improve presentation skills.

In including the testimony of a witness or witnesses into a Management Learning Contract, it is advisable to bear in mind the realistic limits of this form of assessment.

- If the witness is to provide an opinion – whether something was of a sufficient standard, accurate enough, authentic, adhering to company policy, in other words anything more than attesting to factual occurrence – which will often be the case – he/she must be briefed as to the role to be played and criteria to be used.
- It follows that permission should be obtained from the proposed witness to include his/her testimony in the assessment of the MLC.

- Witness opinion should never be the sole means of assessing a contract, although it can often be a part of the assessment.
- The relationship between the witness and the learner/manager should be borne in mind when considering witness testimony: it will be putting too much pressure on subordinates to expect them to provide absolutely truthful testimony which would result in their boss failing an MLC (see Box 6.10). The same may be said of colleagues, and in some cases, bosses, too.

Box 6.10 The governors

Neil proposed to deal with a problem facing his area for one of his MLC's Access points to the network for distributing gas in the area, called governors, had been established in a piece-meal fashion over the years. Only the operator-engineers knew where all the governors were located. In certain circumstances it was important to be able to access the network quickly, and Neil thought that in the longer term a guide-book and record of the governors would be necessary.

His learning objectives concerned acquiring an accurate knowledge of the locations of all the governors in his area, and developing his skills in communication through the preparation of a clear and simple guide.

The clarity and simplicity of the guide, which contained photographs of the locations of all the governors, was evident. The trainer was in no position to assess the accuracy of the contents, however, nor was anyone else – except the operator-engineers, who worked for Neil.

One of the engineers attended part of the assessment. Rather than ask for his opinions on the guide, the trainer first asked him about the governors and his experience of maintaining and visiting them, and recent examples of the need to gain access to them. This enabled him to compile a list of seven or eight governors, which he was able to find set out in the guide. He then moved on to ask for opinions: Did the engineer think the guide was complete? Was it useful? and so on.[*]

The probe for factual information, against which to check the accuracy of the learner/manager's report, provided a better check than simply a straightforward request for an opinion.

[*]*Note*: Of course the engineer said the guide was no use to him, personally, because he already knew where all the governors were.

Personal report

Some form of personal report is likely to make up the bulk of the evidence for assessing a contract. On the due date, the manager/learner may be expected to:

Box 6.11 The hostile witness

On some occasions, bosses become very protective of their subordinates and will intervene when the trainer is asking probing questions or relaying constructive criticism. Where this occurs, the trainer must handle the situation as well as he/she is able at the time, and should then make sure that any future MLCs do not rely on the boss to provide opinions, but specify a factual element in the testimony, or require some constructively critical feedback in the testimony.

A different problem arises when the manager proposes undertaking an MLC in an area where the boss considers, mistakenly, himself to be extremely competent. One manager, Malcolm, proposed to improve his report-writing skills. His boss, Ted, said, 'I think this'll be a good one for him to tackle, I didn't used to be any good at reports myself, but I learned. You have to in this job. What you have to do is: Pad it out.'

The trainer avoided incorporating Ted's evaluation of Malcolm's style in the assessment of the MLC. (See also Chapter 8)

- give an account of what he/she did in pursuit of the contract objectives and what happened as a result of his/her actions , and
- summarise what he/she has learned as a result of this, and
- set out a plan for future action.

Each personal report need not follow this particular structure, of course, but this structure follows part of the pattern of the Learning Circle (it is reflection, knowledge, planning) and is particularly useful when attempting to assess action that cannot be directly witnessed.

The form of the personal report may be either written or oral, and there is much to be said for considering the advantages of each when negotiating the assessment measures.

The requirement to produce specific points in writing can concentrate the mind (e.g., 'a clear and realistic action plan to make further improvements in skill over the next six months', 'a list of the skills I feel are important in interviewing, together with a rating of where I stand in each category'). On the other hand, the requirement to produce a written report can divert significant amounts of effort from the development of the skill itself, and focusses far too much emphasis (and reward) on the skills of report writing to the exclusion of others.

The oral report, on the other hand, enables a to and fro between assessor and learner, saves the learner time, and maintains a focus on what was done and what was learned rather than what has been written about it. The assessor is able to seek the level of detail he/she requires about what the learner did and said.

The Behavioural Event Interview approach (see Chapter 1), of seeking a very detailed account of actions, thoughts and feelings, can form the basis of the oral report.

In general, the written form is appropriate for summary (What have I learned? Where do I still need to develop?) and for outline (a list of the actions I undertook); the oral form is appropriate for the detailed accounts of what I did, the reasons why I feel I have learned the target skills, my rationale for my learning strategy.

Even when the bulk of the MLC can be assessed by demonstration there remains a role for the personal report, to summarise what has been learned, to clarify the objectives of a particular demonstration, to set out the next steps of the action plan (see Box 6.12).

Assessing products and outcomes

As a trainer, you are likely to be invited to assess a contract by its products and outcomes. Products may be useful items of corroborative evidence; the salesplan, the financial analysis, the report recommending a change to current practice. Because managers work through other people, the use of some outcomes as assessment measures may be more difficult.

The junior manager who wishes to learn how to improve his team's morale might offer an improvement in productivity as best measure, and in a similar vein the manager who wishes to develop her counselling skills might suggest improved behaviour by the problem employee in question as the most appropriate yardstick. Marketing skills? Well, can I increase sales? Training skills? Will the trainees learn more quickly? Negotiating skills? Will the other side accept my proposals?

There is a danger in each of these areas, that the behaviour of others, apart from the learner/manager, is being assessed. The assessment might penalise bad luck or reward good luck and in either case overlook the degree of skill that has been developed.

What kind of criteria

Once we have established the type of evidence we seek, we need to agree on how we will know whether or not it meets the necessary standard.

Box 6.12 Assessing outcomes

Dennis originally proposed a project: to prepare a new form for appraising his staff in the laboratory. It was a proposal he was very keen to tackle, so during discussion we uncovered the principal, obvious learning objective: a clear understanding of the criteria for assessing whether the laboratory staff were doing their jobs effectively and efficiently. (Dennis was newly promoted and the laboratory had been re-organised at the same time, so this was not as simple a contract as it may sound).

Assessment measures included Dennis producing the new criteria – set out on a form to be issued in appraisals – and a comparison with the old criteria, and also included the acceptance of the new criteria and the new form by senior management. This last term was proposed by Dennis, and the trainer duly neutralised it, after some discussion (see below).

When it came to assessment, Dennis produced old and new forms, and the new forms met all the criteria, including acceptance by senior management. As his account of what had happened unfolded, however, it seemed that his original proposals had been the focus of some discussion. The Personnel Manager and another member of senior management had made suggestions and amendments. At the end of the day it was difficult to see what parts of the new form were Dennis's and what had come from other people.

With the benefit of hindsight, the problems with this contract arose from its origins as a project. It is good practice to suggest that part of the assessment of such MLCs includes an evaluation by the manager of what he has actually learned (main points in writing). This encourages the reflective and summarising stages of learning which the action and results orientation of the project is prone to overlook.

Neutralising outcome assessments is simply a matter of pointing out the dangers of depending on the actions of other people, and suggesting an addition to the proposed assessment: e.g.

- Sales will increase by five per cent over the period: if not I will be able to explain why.
- The trainers will learn more quickly: if not I will be able to explain what factors are preventing this.

This is a matter of:

- establishing the entry behaviour of the learner/manager: making an accurate assessment of the initial level of skill.
- estimating the degree of difficulty of the proposed contract, and setting this alongside the amount of time available to the learner.
- defining the relevant dimensions of the evidence the manager will produce at the end of the MLC.

There is a certain degree of difficulty for the trainer in each of these three areas.

The establishment of entry behaviour is related to the methods of diagnosis which have been used prior to the contract negotiation, and is closely linked to why the manager wants to undertake the MLC. If the learning area can be clearly defined in terms of specialised skills, such as the use of particular analytic techniques or types of computer programme, for example, it may be easier to see what new dimension the individual is about to explore. It is more difficult when the learning is a matter of a degree of improvement.

Where the manager is not learning a new skill, but improving in a skill already exercised, an initial audit as the first stage of the MLC can serve as a benchmark .

Box 6.13 The starting point

Brian undertook an MLC to improve his contribution to regular company meetings. His proposal is a good example of the type.

Learning objectives:
1. To obtain a clear understanding of the skills needed to make an effective contribution to meetings.
2. To clarify my own strengths and needs in relation to these skills.
3. To develop, through practice, my ability in one high need area.

Brian did some reading and devised his own list of the necessary skills. (If he were doing the MLC today he might use the Performance Criteria for contributing to meetings from the Competence Standards model). He graded himself (0–4) on the skills, and asked his boss to do the same. He then concentrated on one of his areas of need. An assessment six weeks later indicated an improvement, not only in the target area, but in the skills generally. In such a 'soft' area the skills improvement was only measurable through:
- Brian's own perceptions and self-evaluation against the criteria he had chosen.
- Brian's account of occasions when he had demonstrated the skills he claimed to have improved.
- The assessment of his boss against the chosen criteria.

As well as providing a means of measuring improvement through the MLC, it can also indicate aspects of performance that may need special attention.

It is not always possible to establish an accurate, quantified assessment of entry behaviour, but questioning by the trainer at this stage will help to clarify the skill level at which the learner is entering the contract, and may also provide clues which will help to identify the criteria that are most relevant to assessing the MLC.

Estimating the degree of difficulty of the MLC and setting this within a realistic time frame is a fundamental part of the trainer's role. As we saw in Chapter 5, the learner tends to be unrealistic and to overestimate what can be achieved. To probe or to establish the realism of a target the trainer must consider, as well as the learner's entry behaviour, the proposed action plan:

- the various activities, including reflection and evaluation, that make up the plan.
- the amount of time it will take to undertake each one.
- the scheduling of any learning opportunities included in the MLC.
- the desired or proposed schedule of the contract.
- the amount of time available to the learner/manager to undertake the action plan.

Box 6.14 Scheduling

Each of these five aspects of timing should be established by the trainer.

There will probably be a desired (or even fixed) deadline for completion of the MLC. For each activity, the trainer should:

- have a reasonably clear picture of what it entails, and
- ask the manager how long it will take.

This can be set beside the amount of time the manager proposes to spend on the MLC, and any other distractions which are likely to take place (holidays, transfers, predictably high workloads, etc.)

Finally, for any scheduled activities within the MLC – meetings where skills will be practised, training courses where information will be obtained, etc. – the trainer should ask when and/or how often they will take place during the proposed life of the MLC.

An MLC proposal for one manager was, after an hour's discussion, at the final stages of clarifying details: he was going to improve his skills of chairing meetings. Exactly how many of these regular meetings would he chair over the next eight weeks? Four? Three? Two?

In fact, the answer was none, and the negotiation started again with a fresh, blank form.

By questioning in these areas, the trainer can help the manager to establish realistic targets within a given time.

Defining the relevant dimensions of the evidence the manager will produce to prove the MLC has been completed is a mixture of quantifying and agreeing qualitative measures.

For example, the manager might propose to demonstrate his/her increased skill in making formal presentations by giving a presentation on a particular topic, and including the assessor in the audience.

Simply in order to clarify what might be expected, it would be good practice for the trainer to establish agreement on the size of the audience and the length of the presentation.

Secondly, some criteria as to the quality of the presentation, or a means of establishing these criteria, should be agreed.

So, manager and trainer might agree:

- on a set of criteria that are discussed and written in an agreed format when the MLC is drawn up (see Box 6.15) or
- to use a pre-established set of criteria for the skill area from some published source, or
- that the manager will research the area and propose a set of criteria by which the presentation might be judged. These must be realistic in terms of what is generally regarded as competent performance, and must be agreed before the presentation is given.

Box 6.15 A good presentation

Jennifer's Management Learning Contract on improving her presentation skills included the following terms:

The presentation will be assessed on the extent to which:
1. It achieves or can be shown to have pursued its objectives. (The objectives are to be stated to the trainer before the presentation)
2. It is well structured.
3. It keeps the attention of the average member of the audience.
4. Delivery is clear and confident.
5. Visual aids are clear and appropriate, and there are no significant weaknesses in any of these five areas.

Thirdly, some means of establishing what learning or development has taken place should be agreed. The likely form of this will be a type of personal report, comparing previous performance with that demonstrated at the end of the MLC. It is advisable to define some aspects of this report: will it be written or oral? (a written core, at least, is preferable in this case). Must it find some improvement has taken place? (in the context of a Management Learning Contract, it should). What other criteria might be applied? Perhaps only that the report should be credible and convincing, and seek to raise evidence of improvement where possible, rather than relying entirely on assertion.

It may be that witness testimony, in the form of the reactions of the audience at the assessed presentation, and the account of witnesses to previous presentations can be used to corroborate the assessments.

In another case, the main part of the assessment might be by personal report. Without further guidance in this matter, the tendency of the learner/manager is to propose 'A written report' full stop. As we saw earlier in this chapter it is advisable to specify the contents of the report in advance. It is also desirable to make explicit some criteria by which the report will be judged, even if this is no more than, as above, that it is credible and convincing and provides evidence where possible rather relying entirely on assertion (see Box 6.16).

Box 6.16 At one remove

Suppose the presentation we have used as an example were not available for direct assessment and was to be evaluated largely through personal report: what might the criteria be?

1. The report should set out the objectives of the presentation, an outline of content, the proposed structure, and include copies of all visual aids to be used (if practical). The content and structure should be shown to relate to the objectives.

2. The report should set out factual information, covering venue, time, duration of the presentation and numbers in the audience.

3. An account should be given of the presentation indicating any departures from the planned structure, any problems and how they were overcome. An evaluation should be made of whether delivery was clear and confident and whether the presentation kept the attention of the average member of the audience. An action plan for future improvement should be included.

4. The report should cover all the points above. It should be clear and credible.

Conclusions

It may be clear now that the aims of the trainer to ensure that an MLC is realistic, precise and clear are nowhere more important than in the area of assessment. It is crucial to establish a clear picture of the type, the content and the nature of the evidence that will be produced, and to establish explicit agreement on the measures against which it will be assessed.

As a trainer, you have more scope for intervention here than elsewhere in the MLC, for taking the initiative in making proposals and for suggesting alternatives to the ideas put forward by the learner/manager. But if you wish to make full use of the potential of the MLC approach, you must remember that you do not have a free hand. Assessment measures must be agreed with the manager, not imposed without consent, and you must be careful not to change the MLC out of all recognition by incorporating radical proposals at the assessment stage.

Assessing MLCs

A number of factors will affect how assessment of an MLC is carried out. Among them are:

- the consequences of successful completion (for example, certification, or recognition within the company).
- who is entitled to assess – whether it is the trainer, an external assessor, a senior manager or a panel.

This section is written on the basis of experience with management development programmes where consequences do follow on the successful completion of an MLC, and this makes the role of assessor more important than it would otherwise be. Where there are no extrinsic consequences following on the completion of a contract, the only reward is an enhanced skill or improved self-image, and the only function of assessment measures is to provide the individual with a precise target for self-evaluation. The role of the trainer in this assessment – if there is a role at all – is one of helper and counsellor, with no effective voice in the judgement. This is similar to the situation in the Action Plans referred to at the beginning of this chapter.

In what follows, it is assumed that assessment is carried out by a trainer. In Chapter 8 the involvement of the learner/manager's boss is examined.

The actual business of assessment will vary from contract to contract depending on what has been agreed. The trainer, acting as assessor, might move from being part of the audience at a presentation, to a seat in front of a VDU where a manager is demonstrating new-found programming skills, to an office where a manager provides the written report that concludes an MLC. The only advice relevant to all of these situations is that the trainer should have a clear idea of what was agreed as assessment measures, and should keep a copy of the written agreement in sight during the assessment. The fundamental aim of the trainer at this stage is to make a fair and accurate assessment of the contract.

A component of most assessments is a discussion between assessor and learner, either because an oral account or an interview was agreed, or in order to clarify some aspects of a demonstration or a written report. Obviously the trainer, as assessor, must listen carefully to what the manager has to say.

There will be a need to ask some questions to clarify matters, and some feedback in the form of an assessment of the manager's progress will be expected.

Asking questions

Here, just as much as in the negotiation stage, the trainer's role should be one of questioning the manager, and encouraging that person to think and speak. It is generally advisable to acknowledge whatever documentation is at hand: in most cases, this will be the written MLC agreement (in some cases a written report may have been submitted in advance of the meeting), and then to pass the initiative over to the learner/manager with an open question such as: 'How did it go?'

The most common need for questions is to:

- obtain more information about events or activities the manager undertook as part of the contract (see Box 6.17).
- assess the extent to which the manager has evaluated events and actions: typically we might ask: 'What makes you think you have improved?' or simply 'What have you actually learned?'
- assess the realism of any action plans produced as part of the MLC. Typically, we might ask: 'How will that work?'
- guide the manager's account so that it covers all the assessment measures, or so that it focusses upon an area of particular interest in the MLC. The written agreement (and any evidence already

made available – such as a written report, or a demonstration) can be used as the basis for these questions.

Box 6.17 Tell me about it

Frank undertook an MLC to improve his counselling skills. As part of the contract, he proposed to carry out two counselling interviews with problem employees and evaluate his own performance. He provided a written report of what he had done and how he felt he had developed, but the interviews were dealt with briefly, in a summarised paragraph or two, and the trainer had no real impression of what had happened.

In discussion with Frank, the trainer said: 'I'm trying to get a clear picture of what happened in those interviews. Tell me about one of them. How did it start?' Using a Behavioural Event approach, which asks the respondent to go into detail about actions, words, thoughts and feelings, the trainer got Frank to reconstruct parts of the interview: where it took place, where each man was sitting, how Frank began the discussion and so on. (In this case the strict focus of the BE approach on the actual event was not maintained throughout the discussion, as Frank was asked to evaluate his performance with the benefit of hindsight.)

It became evident from the detailed account that the interviews bore only a slight resemblance to those counselling interviews where employees discuss their difficulties with a manager. This was not apparent from the written report.

Sometimes probing for specific facts is the best method of penetrating the gloss of the written word or the smooth oral presentation. How long did the interviews last? Did either man say that he had a problem he wished to discuss? were key questions in this case.

Giving feedback

The trainer will be expected to provide some feedback on the manager's performance under the MLC. This will include making an assessment, and may go quite a way beyond.

Making an assessment may range from a simple agreement that the manager has achieved the objectives of the contract, to a summary of what the manager has produced and an evaluation of this against agreed, or implicit, criteria. The more simple and straightforward the MLC, the more simple the assessment can be. With more complex contracts, where the results may be difficult to measure, it is appropriate to summarise and to relate the results to explicit criteria.

This may involve some constructive criticism where the results of the MLC appear to fall short of good practice, even though the MLC as a whole will be judged to be complete.

Box 6.18 Delivering judgement

When a discussion has been in progress for some time, and the manager has given an account of what was done, and made some points in support of the case for a favourable assessment, and a range of assessment measures were agreed for the MLC, the satisfactory conclusion of the meeting calls for someone to summarise, to check if each assessment measure has been satisfied and to comment on areas of over- and under-achievement, and that role often falls to the trainer.

To make it clear that the business of assessment is taken seriously, it is good practice to refer to agreed criteria: 'We agreed that the reports you would produce at the end of the MLC would be clear, accurate and well-structured: and we've agreed that they are.' It is rare for all the criteria on which we make judgement to be specified exhaustively in advance, and additional points may express implicit criteria, e.g. 'I must add that the way in which the reports have been set out makes them very appealing and easy to read' or 'I must say that positive aspects of the reports are somewhat let down by the presentation. How would you improve that?'

Giving feedback may also involve:

- *Congratulating* managers on their achievements, where this is appropriate, and encouraging them to evaluate and value what they have done.
- *Empathising with* managers on occasions when they have found the MLC difficult, or have come face to face with unpleasant truths about themselves.
- *Stretching* managers by encouraging them to look beyond the MLC they have just completed. If an MLC is a specific, targeted piece of self-development, deliberately limited to a few rungs on the ladder, it seems appropriate to point out, in an encouraging manner, the further heights that could be scaled.

Incomplete contracts

So far we have made the comfortable assumption that we are assessing MLCs that, in the end, we will agree have been successfully completed. That will probably not always be the case. For one reason or another, on the date set for assessment some managers will not be able to show that they have reached all the agreed measures of assessment.

The choice is between two options – or a combination incorporating elements of each:

- to allow more time for the manager to complete the MLC and furnish the necessary evidence – *to refer the MLC.*

- to agree on changes to parts or all of the contract – in other words, *to revise the MLC.*

Referring the MLC may be the most appropriate option when the contract has been delayed, in part or in whole, but the manager is still confident that it can be completed. The trainer should be sure to establish a new deadline, and to explore the likelihood of the factor which caused the original delay continuing to disrupt progress. If further problems are a distinct possibility, it may be better to revise the relevant section of the agreement.

Referral may well be the best approach where a manager has simply overlooked an agreed assessment measure and failed to provide a piece of evidence, or has provided inadequate or unconvincing evidence in relation to a particular measure. In the latter case, it is good practice to discuss, agree and specify precisely what is required to complete the contract.

Each assessment is an occasion when precedents are set, of course. The trainer who makes a lenient assessment of one manager's MLC to avoid conflict with him may run into trouble with other managers who feel their honest efforts have been devalued by the allowances made for their colleague.

Revising the MLC may be a matter of making marginal changes, or a complete re-negotiation. It is the best option when the contract is frustrated through a change of circumstances, and part of the original agreement is no longer possible. It appears to be the most appropriate choice, too, when the MLC has been much more involved, or more difficult, or larger than was ever envisaged.

Box 6.19 Referred and revised agreements

Four examples of MLCs that failed because of dependencies on unreliable factors were given in the previous chapter (Box 5.2. above).

In the case of Eileen and the delayed computer equipment, the MLC was shelved and a new agreement, in a different skill area, was made. When the equipment was finally installed and working, eight weeks late, Eileen still wanted to undertake the MLC which was on the shelf. With no amendments, other than to the deadline date, she completed it successfully.

Colin depended on having a supervisor to observe and coach for two months, but the man was transferred after a month. In this case, the MLC was revised by agreement so that Colin's self-evaluation was based on the two meetings attended, rather than the four planned. This was not ideal, but appeared to be the best option in an unfortunate situation.

Box 6.19 continued

Louise who, rather like Eileen, found her computing contract delayed – this time by a delayed start to a short training course – was able to find a similar solution: the original MLC was finally undertaken at a later date.

Patricia, who was going to practice being assertive in a series of particular meetings, found herself frustrated when the meetings were re-organised and her attendance was no longer required. The MLC was revised to focus on behaving assertively in other sets of circumstances Patricia was finding difficult.

Finally, another case of necessary revision was David's MLC. He wanted to be able to use a particular computerised graphics package to improve the impact of his presentations, and he undertook to produce a twenty-minute presentation that would include five mobile graphics.

Near to the time for assessment of the results he telephoned the trainer and confessed that the MLC was only partially complete. A little over half the presentation was finished, and only three mobile graphics. But he had by then spent over 120 hours working on the presentation (and the notional length of his MLC was only 40 hours). Under the circumstances, and after witnessing a demonstration of David's proficiency with keyboard and screen, the trainer, suggested the MLC be revised and considered complete.

In keeping with the imperative that the MLC should belong to the individual manager, it is good practice for the trainer to offer the manager the option to negotiate a new contract when the original agreement runs into difficulties.

Where marginal changes are made to an MLC which is substantially complete the trainer should bear in mind the warning, above, about creating precedents, and be sure that the grounds on which the revisions are being made are clearly stated and appear fair.

Any revisions, whether major or marginal, should be in writing, as with the original agreement, and copies made for both parties.

Summary

In this chapter we have considered a number of ways in which a Management Learning Contract may be assessed.

The trainer can exercise more influence in suggesting and defining terms at the assessment stage than at any other point in the MLC. Precision and realism are very important here. Care should be taken that the manager still feels ownership of the MLC.

Evidence of successful completion might take the form of:

- a demonstration in the work-place.
- a demonstration in conditions that simulate those of the work-place.
- tape recordings – video or audio – of performance. These might provide supporting evidence, as might
- witness testimony.

There will usually be call for a personal report to describe and evaluate what has been done, and to explain what has been learned.

Criteria should be made explicit where possible, to set out agreed quantities or qualities against which success of the MLC will be judged.

In assessing the MLC, the trainer will usually be involved in a discussion with the learner/manager. The trainer's role is to make a fair and accurate assessment of performance through:

- examining evidence
- asking questions
- giving feedback

and, if necessary, agreeing to

- refer the MLC and/or
- revise the terms of the MLC.

Exercise

1. What kind of evidence would you suggest to assess an MLC in each of the following areas?
    (a) Coaching Skills
    (b) Developing my Proactivity
    (c) Becoming more Assertive
    (d) Report Writing

2. In each case, what criteria would you use?

Chapter 7

The role of the trainer

When you have completed this chapter you should be able to:

- **identify the various roles a trainer might play in supporting and using MLCs on a management development programme.**
- **establish what you might do to introduce and support MLCs in your company.**
- **recognise good and bad practice in questions and statements made by a trainer negotiating or assessing a contract.**

Introduction

Trainers are asked to fulfil a number of roles. Any one individual may be called upon to fulfil all of them as part of his/her job or, by accident or design, may specialise in only one or two. The task of negotiating and assessing Management Learning Contracts must be seen in the context of the other functions the trainer – or, at least, the training department – must perform, for they are important to the success of the MLCs.

The main concern of this chapter, however, is the role of the trainer in negotiation and assessment: the skills that are needed, the approaches to take, the means of self-development. It is assumed that you have made a careful reading of the two previous chapters and that, although you may have a question or two about some points of detail, you have understood what you have read. This chapter should address some of the unfinished points of detail.

The trainer roles

The roles of trainers may be set into five broad areas (see Fig 7.1). The amount of time any particular trainer spends on each role will depend upon the demands of his/her job.

Designer

This involves planning the structure and content of any training and development programme whether on a grand or on a small scale. It may be a social process – indeed, if it is large in scale it will almost certainly involve other people. It may involve studying, or making use of studies of, training and development needs. It may entail exploring the requirements of accrediting bodies. To some extent it will involve absorbing information about what is required, what is available, what is happening elsewhere, and putting together a coherent plan for a programme.

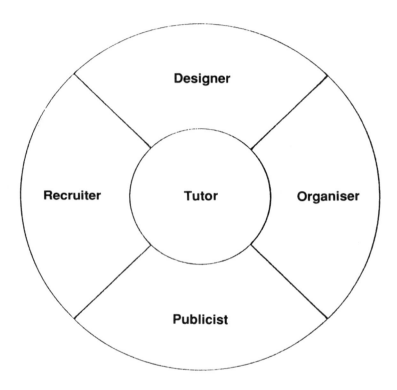

Figure 7.1 The trainer roles

Organiser

This involves making available resources to support the training programme: acquiring the necessary books, computing equipment, room-space, buffet lunches, tutors, visiting speakers. Many people who are identified as trainers within their organisations spend most of their time in the Organiser role: obtaining and spending a budget in the best possible way to support other trainers and tutors who work more directly with learners/managers.

Publicist

This involves publicising particular programmes, and the work of the training and development department more generally. It may take the trainer into the business of designing posters, leaflets and articles for the house magazine. It may take him/her to conferences with trainers from other organisations. Or it may simply involve sending messages along well-used internal channels to line managers.

Recruiter

This involves reaching agreement with applicants or nominations to a particular programme. It may involve a careful scrutiny of the individual applicant. It may involve a careful balancing of internal organisational political pressures. For internal courses it may be a role the trainer avoids but where there is a shortage of places, or a shortage of funds, in relation to the number of applicants, some form of assessment, of recruitment and selection, needs to be made. (We might include here the screening role that training departments, as budget-holders, exercise regarding applicants to external courses.)

Tutor

This involves working with people on training and development programmes and helping them to learn. It would include any briefing related to learning processes (but not the welcome to the facility or to the course which the trainer as Organiser or Publicist might extend). Thereafter it might include directive lecturing, workshop facilitation, organising role plays, steering the analysis of outdoor activities, negotiating Management Learning Contracts and so on. People training as Tutors will have special expertise and preferences for certain styles of approach and specific subject areas. We should include assessment here, as a potential part of this role.

What do the trainer roles look like in relation to Management Learning Contracts?

Design

Certain key decisions need to be taken about the overall design of the programme. Who will it be for? How long will it last? What will it contain? Some exposition or explanation of theories or facts seems to be necessary in addition to the use of MLCs – even if this is just to explain:

- a model of good practice.
- a means of self-diagnosis.
- how the MLC method will work.

If some form of external accreditation (see Box 7.1) is sought, the design of the programme and the means by which people are assessed need to fit with the guidelines of the awarding body.

Box 7.1 Designing the programme

A logical programme design provides for a mixture of workshop/classroom activities – to brief and debrief, to explore the ideas and frameworks and to formulate plans, and then later to discuss and evaluate actions – and also periods when it is possible to undertake actions in the workplace.

This indicates a programme structure of:

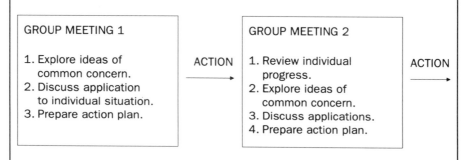

The commitment to take action between the group meetings must be emphasised by the trainer, and the review of individual progress should reinforce this.

The initial 'common concerns' may be guessed by the trainer ('What is a Competent Manager?'; 'Time Management'; 'Better Decisions'; 'Working in Teams') and thereafter may be established by group consensus.

The length of time of the group meeting, and of the intervening Action Time, is another design decision. If new ideas of any substance are to be explored, the group meeting can hardly be shorter than half a day, and a full day may be preferable. More detailed workshop activity may take group meetings of several days in duration.

The length of the Action Time between meetings must be balanced against a number of factors. Two months seems an outside length if a detailed MLC is to be achieved, unless trainer support is given to individuals in the interim: three weeks seems to be the shortest reasonable amount of time to allow if anything of respectable size is to be undertaken.

For programmes for junior manager and supervisory levels, the Business and Technician Education Council and the Institute of Supervisory Management are both accessible organisations, and for any programme that is to last more than six months the additional incentive of recognition of efforts through accreditation is attractive to managers (see Box 7.2).

Box 7.2 Accreditation

BTEC and ISM set out guidelines as to what a learner should demonstrate, and what a programme should cover in order to be recognised. Both institutions are very keen to see company-led schemes and employer involvement. Any large company with a training department of a reasonable size will probably have enough resources to establish accredited programmes.

Both institutions are committed to maintaining certain standards, of course, and clear proposals of programme strategy and content, learning processes, resources, and assessment measures, need to be submitted for approval. The approval processes take time, and it is not wise to gamble on approval being given at the first time of asking.

If the training department has no experience of these matters, it may be worth while working in partnership with a local college for the first year, or hiring an adviser from a college. (Make sure the people you are hiring have experience of taking proposals to the relevant institution before you hire them. And when you do hire them, follow their advice.)

Alternatively, internal recognition and company certificates might be considered. This will involve clear decisions about how 'success' on the programme will be assessed: how many pieces of work (completed contracts)?; over what time period?; who will assess?

For the MLCs themselves, decisions need to be taken about the rules: the range of possible learning areas, the length and size, etc. (see above, Box 5.1). Decisions should be taken about the materials needed to brief and to support contracts, and about whether support groups will operate during the lifetime of an MLC (see below, 'Support').

Organisation

A certain amount of detailed work on times and resources is necessary: the trainers who will act to recruit learners/managers, and tutor them, must be identified and their availability cleared: the printed materials for briefing programme members (and perhaps their line managers) need to be prepared: there are rooms to be booked, and dates secured in the diaries of all concerned.

As mentioned above (see Box 4.2) evidence of organisational interest and support, in the form of expenditure on the launch of a programme, and the expectation of a formal review of its success, can act as strong motivators to programme participants. These events need careful organisation to succeed.

Publicity

Some publicity work may be necessary to launch the first programme. If it is a radical departure from what has gone before, the trainer's first need will probably be to sell the idea to senior management. Of course, in doing so the trainer will know that the attractions of the MLC approach and the supporting programme will be different for each group, i.e. for senior managers, line managers of learners, and potential learners/managers themselves, it is necessary to emphasise certain different key features to publicise the programme effectively .

Box 7.3 Sales pitches

Everyone should appreciate the fact that training and development will become more relevant.

Learners/managers should appreciate the amount of choice they as individuals are offered, and the way in which they can receive help and advice in tackling real problems at work.

(Some) line managers will appreciate the opportunity to be involved in influencing training and development, particularly if the firm supporting structure to help them do this is emphasised. They will appreciate the fact that, as learning takes place at work they will not lose the services of the learner for long or for regular periods of time on block or day release.

Senior management will appreciate this last point, too, and may be more enthusiastic than the line managers about the line manager involvement in agreeing and assessing the MLCs. Senior management may be more supportive of the learning approach that offers returns in the middle rather than the short term, than line managers.

Management concerns will also vary from company to company, and it goes without saying that the astute trainer as Publicist will be aware of this. Obviously, it is unproductive to emphasise the scope that MLCs provide for line managers to become really involved in designing the development of their juniors if the main concern of senior management is the seriously high level of demands on the time of line managers.

Recruitment

Because of the self-driven nature of the MLC approach, it is important for learners/managers to be voluntary applicants to the programme, and to be able to make some reasonable statement about what they want to learn. There are, unfortunately, still too many cases of people being sent on training programmes by bosses who expect some miracle cure to be wrought. Recruitment should stress personal commitment and responsibility.

Box 7.4 Recruitment criteria

Examples of suggested criteria for recruitment for a management development programme which requires some commitment of time outside of working hours, and leads to a qualification are:

1. *Motivation and concerns of the individual*
The manager must want to enrol on the programme. The best motivation is that of a person searching for a better way to meet job and career demands and concerned also to obtain a qualification. Indications of self-awareness and open-mindedness are desirable, as are indications that the person is a learner/doer.

2. *Commitment of individual*
Evidence of an ability to see things through, despite difficulties or resistance, is desirable. Avoid known apologists.

Beware of willing volunteers who have no real perception of what the programme entails, including time commitment. Participants may need to put aside a more preferred activity to meet this time commitment.

3. *Role of individual*
Some freedom of action and influencing role is essential. Managerial or supervisory responsibilities are desirable.

4. *Time in post*
Six months minimum.

5. *Stability of environment*
Re-organisation has a bad effect on pacing, as do sudden shifts or peaks in workload. If these are likely over the 12 month period then proceed with caution.

If this is the first programme within the company which has used the MLC approach, (and especially if this represents a significant departure from what has happened in the past) the trainer as Recruiter would be wise to take the usual precautions and to look for safer, rather than riskier, course members until the training team have been through the whole programme once and have ironed out the inevitable bugs in the design. This gives the programme a chance of being established as a success, and enhances motivation and confidence in the method all round.

Tutoring

We have seen, over the last three chapters, some of the challenges facing the trainer in using MLCs. Careful decisions need to be taken about who will negotiate and assess the MLCs and how they will train for this. Just as important are the decisions and the organisation of the Priming and Diagnosis. If there is no planning and organising of this preparatory stage to the contract, the trainer is likely to be faced with a difficult, up-hill struggle against confusion and a plethora of project proposals.

Training for the challenge of negotiating and assessing MLCs will involve at least acquiring an understanding of the basic principles, agreeing and carrying out a successful contract oneself, and negotiating and assessing some practice contracts with others (see below, 'Training the trainers').

We can draw together at this stage some of the points we have made about the trainer's role in the previous two chapters and extend them in a practical, detailed manner. Let us do so by separating the stages of involvement into Negotiation, Support and Assessment.

Negotiation

The aims of the trainer, as we saw in Chapter 5, are to achieve an agreement that is realistic, precise and clear, and owned by the learner/manager – and to do this at a reasonable cost.

In order to achieve the ownership objective, it is important to abandon the predominantly telling and directing role, which is the principal style of some trainers, and to ask a great many questions. If every statement you make is a question, however, the manager will feel on the defensive before long, the discussion may become aimless or circular, and the strain of making everything dependent on the sought opinion of the other party will soon tell on you, too.

There is a need to find a balance between asking for and providing information. Some people feel comfortable in the role after only a short exposure: others take a little while to find their feet. The analysis that follows may be helpful in fault-finding and in making improvements.

Questions

Questions are used for three separate purposes in negotiating MLCs. You should use more questions than any other type of statement, both in negotiation and in assessment.

1. **To find out:** questions are used to get more information about the proposal, the reasons for the proposal and the existing level of skill or knowledge of the manager.

In particular, it is good practice to make sure you have an accurate understanding of the proposal itself. Simple questions are necessary, based on the written proposal, for example:

'What do you mean by "interview people"?'
'What do you mean by "interviewing skills"?'
'How long will this take?'
'How many people will you interview?'
'Where will you do the work?'

These questions serve two important purposes:

- they enable you to establish a clear picture of the MLC in your own mind, such that you can think more easily about its realism, about what support may be needed, and about what assessment is appropriate.
- they establish a clearer picture in the mind of the manager about what he/she is going to do. Interspersed with guidance from you and decisions from the manager, they will lead to a more precise contract – which has a greater motivational effect on the manager who undertakes it.

Box 7.5 Precision and motivation

Work on trainer training in particular highlights the importance of specific targets as a means of motivating and measuring learners who are using MLCs.

One such contract had as an activity:
- to record a series of time logs

which was to be carried forward into assessment as:
- comparison of daily time logs.

Experience shows that it is essential to make a more precise statement at this point, and to specify the number of days the learner will log. Not only does this need to be precise, but also realistic: learners/managers who wildly propose to keep detailed daily logs for every day of the next six weeks must gently be dissuaded from doing so in most cases. The task is unrealistic. On the third day they will give up.

The point and purpose of the comparison should also be defined: what was it designed to reveal?

The written word of the MLC, quite apart from its value in legislating for matters of assessment, can crystallise and target certain actions and results, and can act in natural and positive ways on the learner's motivation to succeed.

We saw in Chapter 5 that proposals are sometimes problematic, and in such cases the questions are not simply designed to clarify details but to uncover the overall shape of what may be an unclear proposal, or to act as part of a challenge to the project orientation:

'What are you actually going to learn?'.

These questions cover the What, How, When, Where, Who of the proposal, and also the How big, How many, How often, How long issues to establish the dimensions of the MLC.

Box 7.6 The appraisal scheme

James presented his first MLC proposal in a direct and clear manner: he wanted to improve his skills in assessing people who worked for him. To this end, he proposed to set up an appraisal system and to operate it for the eight weeks of the contract, and then report on the skills he had developed.

James had a responsible job as the manager of a day-care centre for a local authority. His line manager was not interested in the management development programme, and did not get involved in discussing the contracts.

Was there an appraisal scheme in the centre at present? asked the trainer.
No, there was not.
How many people worked in the centre?
About thirty-five.
And how many of them would the scheme cover?
Oh, all of them.
Were they all doing the same kind of jobs?
No. There was a wide variety of jobs. The staff were spread across seven or eight different grades, because of an historical anomaly. This contract might sort that out, too.
Was there a trade union?
Most of them were NALGO members. (NALGO was opposed to appraisal schemes.)
Were there clear job descriptions to work from?
No. That would all need doing.

At this point the trainer voiced the opinion that this was a very large contract indeed, and perhaps the way forward was to break it into manageable pieces. What would be the first step? It would be to establish clear job specifications. Had James done that before? James had not. He began an MLC on job analysis. By the time he reached the end he realised that his original vision of operating an appraisal system was a 12 month project, not an eight week contract.

It is also valuable to make some exploration of the reasons for a contract proposal, and the reasons for any of the proposed activities which may not be immediately obvious. This is to guard against the problems that arise when a manager jumps to conclusions about the skills he/she needs to develop in order to solve a problem.

A word of warning: as far as you, the trainer, are concerned it should be the manager's right to propose an MLC in an area he/she thinks fit. Unless you are prepared to risk threatening the manager's sense of ownership of the MLC, and his/her confidence in it, you should restrict questions about motivation to those sufficient to guard against the problems of the Wrong Solution.

Box 7.7 Do you really want to do this?

Probing and querying the reasons why a learner has picked a particular skill area is a recipe for a long discussion which may not produce a choice any better than the initial proposal.

All manner of doubts can surround the beginning of the MLC.

For example, as learner/manager I may decide to improve my ability to make a good first impression: to appear positive, in control and organised.

There may be some doubts in my mind as to:

- whether I can do this. Aren't confident managers born, not made?
- whether I can trust you, the trainer, with the disclosure that I wish I could be more self-confident, positive, etc.
- whether other areas of development might not really be of a higher priority (but I can only choose one!).

To some extent the fear of the challenge, the fear of disclosure, the fear of making the wrong choice, can affect every contract proposal and unless there are very good reasons why a manager should not go ahead with the original suggestion it should not be questioned too closely. Managers can learn a great deal by tackling a contract in slightly the wrong area, and being brought face to face with this. As long as they have been responsible for choosing the contract, they may reflect upon their own choices and self-evaluations.

Finally, it is important to make some exploration of the manager's initial level of competence, in order to gauge the height of appropriate assessment measures. Good questions are:

'What is new about this?'
'What do you expect to learn?'
'What will you be able to do at the end of this contract that you can't do now?'
'What aspect of that skill will you increase during this contract?'
'How will you know you have improved that skill?'
'Is there any way you could prove that you can do that better?'

Clarifying, probing questions are:

> 'Haven't you done this before?'
> 'Isn't this old ground for you?'
> 'What do you know about (computing) now?'

It is best, as always, to begin with the more open, inviting questions and move to the probes later, if necessary.

2. **To acknowledge responsibility:** you will certainly need to ask questions to acknowledge the manager's ownership of, and responsibility for, the MLC. These are simple questions:

> 'What do you want to do, Frank?'
> 'What are you going to learn?'
> 'Which do you prefer?'

The only difficulty experienced here, by trainers who are comfortable with a more directive style, is that of sitting firmly on their own preferences and passing the decision to the learner/manager.

Occasionally, with indecisive or ill-prepared managers, the trainer must be ready to endure long silences following these questions.

3. **To guide:** you will find a use for questions in guiding managers to explore possibilities, where it is more appropriate to ask than to command.

In particular, a questioning approach to dependencies can be helpful:

> 'What if the meetings are cancelled?'
> 'What will you do if you can't get a copy of the book?'
> 'What if the training course doesn't run?'

This non-directional guidance makes the learner/manager consider contingency plans.

The process of considering the possibility that this may not work out precisely according to the original simple plan is a beneficial one.

Discussing even basic contingency plans is one step nearer towards putting them into action, if necessary (see Box 7.8).

A questioning approach can be an effective means of guiding the manager on issues of the size of the proposed MLC:

> 'Is it necessary to do this?'
> 'Will you be able to do all this in the time available?'
> 'What will this assessment measure demonstrate?'

Box 7.8 Habla español?

One trainer, on a programme for training trainers in the use of MLCs, proposed to brush up on her rusty Spanish. Part of her action plan involved reading a Spanish newspaper every day.[*] She assumed that the college, her employer, would take Spanish newspapers.

The contract was a failure. When the time for evaluation came she was unable to show any improvement in her Spanish. One of the reasons she put foward was that the college library did not take Spanish newspapers. And, she declared, the only other source of Spanish newsprint was a newsagent that seemed to specialise in soft porn magazines, and she refused to spend time or money there.

Two days later I noticed a selection of foreign newspapers at the friendly confectionary-newsagent-tobacconist kiosk a hundred yards from the college gates: French, German, Italian, and Spanish.

The contract might have been rescued – or at least made more robust – by a challenge to the unspoken assumption:

'Where will you get a Spanish newspaper?'
'The college library will take one.'
'Are you sure?'
'I haven't actually seen one there. But they must do. We have a language department.'
'What if you can't get one there?'

This question opens up the possible contingency of needing to make an intelligent search of local newsagents, and re-negotiating the contract if there is no success.

[*]*Note*: It may also have helped to make the target more precise. Reading at least one article a day of more than 200 words in length would have been a more precise (and more reasonable) target. In this case one newspaper could have provided enough reading to last a week.

---

are all questions leading to a scaling-down of the proposal, whereas:

'Would that be enough to show you have reached that objective?'
'Would there be time to fit in another interview?'

suggest that more should be put into the proposal (see Box 7.9).

Similarly, a questioning approach to the types of evidence used for assessment is sensible:

'Will anyone from the company be with you when you make this sales presentation?'
'Is there anyone who could evaluate the marketing plan you'll put forward?'

'Is it possible to produce copies of the agendas of the meetings?'

Box 7.9 Questions and statements

It is possible to convey roughly the same meaning in questions and statements, but some of the nuances are important in the MLC agreement.

> 'Is it necessary to do this?'

can be translated as

> 'I don't think (or I'm not sure) it's necessary to do this.'

which can be translated as

> 'It's not necessary to do this.'

We've missed out a number of stages here, including the more challenging question, 'What makes you think it's necessary to do this?' and the more humble statement, 'I may be wrong, but I'm not sure we need to do this.'

From the first question to the final, flat statement, we are doing two things:

- reducing the likelihood of the manager volunteering information,
- reducing the ownership and control the manager may feel for the MLC.

In the same way we could render:

> 'Will you be able to do all this in the time available?'

as

> 'I don't think you'll be able to do all this.'

and

> 'Would there be time to fit in another interview?'

as

> 'You need to carry out at least one more interivew.'

with similar results.

In each of these cases, the question prompts not only a factual answer but also an offer (or consideration of an offer) of a contingency plan, of an alteration to the scale of the contract, of a form of evidence (see Box 7.10).

Generally a questioning approach fits the role and objectives of the trainer in using Management Learning Contracts. It acknowledges the responsibility of the manager; it helps him/her to explore and refine the contract proposal; it presents recommendations and guidance in a suitably respectful form.

Box 7.10 The question spiral?

Of course, using questions to guide the manager does not always result in a quick and simple solution:

Trainer: Is there anyone who could evaluate the marketing plan you'll put foward?
Manager: What, you want someone else to evaluate the plan?
Trainer: Well, d'you think that would be a good idea?
Manager: If you want it evaluated, I suppose.
Trainer: It is part of the contract. I can't evaluate it.
Manager: I suppose the marketing manager could evaluate it, if you want that doing.
Trainer: How do you feel about the marketing manager doing that?

Some managers, as in this case, are reluctant to take control and respond to interventions by trying to seek out the trainer's preferences rather than express their own.

It is, of course, insufficient: trainers need from time to time to make other statements in the course of negotiating an MLC.

Other statements

The negotiation of a Management Learning Contract is a fluid affair, where explorations of objectives, action plan and assessment may take place in no systematic order, and where questions to uncover information are interspersed with questions used to guide the manager, and with other statements from the trainer. For the purposes of explanation and analysis we can divide these other statements into categories, and consider their proper use. In practice they are likely to mingle with the flow of questions from the trainer in the course of the discussion.

1. Directions

A direction is a clear statement of a rule, for example:

> 'The MLC must be about some aspect of managing – not to do with the technical side of your job.'
> 'This is a project, not a learning contract. In using MLCs we are concerned with what you are going to learn, not what you are going to do.'
> 'We must agree the contract before you set about doing it. You can't write up the targets after you have achieved them: that's not acceptable.' (See Box 7.11.)

Box 7.11 Can I have it in writing?

There is a predictable resistance to providing the trainer with a copy of the written contract agreement, such that it is good practice to make sure you leave the meeting with a copy of the form. If it is only a draft, well and good – the manager can forward a neat copy later: in the meantime what you have in your hand stands as the contract. The alternative is to reconcile yourself to chasing up a certain percentage of managers who will omit to provide you with a copy of the form.

The MLC approach provides great flexibility within a supporting structure. It is part of the trainer's role to remind others of the shape of the structure, and the limits of flexibility, and this at times requires clear statements with no promise of movement or compromise.

It is sometimes necessary for trainers new to the MLC approach to mark out the boundaries of the areas where they can make directive statements and still remain effective negotiators.

2. Recommendations

A recommendation is a suggestion about a course of action a manager might take. Of course, advice on action might be phrased as guiding questions:

> 'Have you thought about practising this in team meetings?'
> 'Would it be possible to involve other members of the team in giving feedback?'

Alternatively, as recommendations:

> 'Perhaps you could practise this in team meetings.'
> 'You need to practise this in some way. Perhaps you could use the team meetings.'
> 'If you could involve other members of the team, and get their feedback, it would be helpful.'

One of the roles of the trainer here may be to recommend books, videotapes or other sources of information which may help the manager, or to recommend techniques he/she could try.

Trainers new to negotiating MLCs should be careful not to slip too gratefully into the familiar trainer role of recommender/ lecturer/expert/fount of wisdom at this point, under the guise of providing legitimate advice about resources. Make the recommendation and then seek out the next question to ask.

A way of monitoring your own behaviour, to guard against

exercising undue influence, is to check the words you use in making the recommendation:

> 'You could read/do/try this.'
> 'This might be helpful.'

leave more scope for choice than the loaded

> 'You should read/do/try this.'
> 'You must . . .'
> 'You ought to . . .'

This is not to legislate against vehemence or firm recommendations. If someone proposes to develop interviewing skills then they *should* do more than read books about interviews; if someone is going to claim an increased skill in computer analysis then they *should* be able to demonstrate it. But since a concern of the trainer is for the manager to exercise choice, and to make proposals for a contract, unconscious or undue emphasis on the parental imperatives of 'should', 'must' and 'ought' should be avoided.

3. Options
Less directive than a recommendation, a summary of the options open to a manager can be helpful in progressing the discussion.

For example, a typical response to a broad skills proposal may be:

> 'I can see two learning areas here: the interviewing and the design of the forms. Which is most important to you?'
> 'It seems to me there are two areas here: the training and the marketing. From what you've said, either one of them could make a contract on its own. I think we need to decide which one we're going to go for.'

Options shade into recommendations when there is no explicit choice between alternatives:

> 'You could, of course, use the meetings to practise those skills.'
> 'There are books and courses on stress management, if you want to follow that up as an MLC.'

4. Summaries and observations
Summaries are useful here, as in any situation when people are meeting to discuss complex issues. Summaries of what has been said; summaries of what you, as the trainer, understand, summaries of what has been agreed: these are all valuable. Summaries ensure that

progress is made, and that one eye is kept on the objectives of the MLC.

Observations are simply statements about what appears to be happening:

> 'You don't look too sure.'
> 'This seems important to you.'

or simple statements of fact

> 'I can't assess a contract on speaking French.'
> 'I could use a cup of coffee.'

Summaries and observations are generally neutral statements, leading in to a question.

5. Feelings: confirmations, concerns and preferences

It is helpful to recognise and refer to feelings when negotiating a contract.

Box 7.12 The effective negotiator

Negotiators of MLCs can benefit from some research into negotiations in other spheres. Neil Rackham and John Carlisle made a study of the differences in the behaviours between 'skilled' and 'average' negotiators in industrial relations and commercial matters.

It is relevant to the MLC situation that skilled negotiators spend more time on:

- seeking information
- summaries
- tests of mutual understanding
- commentaries on their own feelings

than 'average' negotiators.

(Rackham and Carlisle 1978).

Confirmations are displays of understanding, agreement and empathy:

> 'I know it can be difficult to do this.'
> 'I can see why you want to do something about it.'
> 'I understand the problem'.

They may encourage the manager to feel more comfortable, to relax a little, to say more.

During the manager's explanation of the proposal, non-verbal confirmations – the nod of the head, the regular eye-contact, the 'uh-huh' sounds that say 'I am listening' – help to support and encourage. The absence of any such confirmation, combined with the questions which are a necessary part of the trainer's role, can create an atmosphere some managers would find inhibiting and almost intimidating.

When an MLC has been agreed, encouraging statements such as:

> 'This looks like a good contract.'
> 'I'm looking forward to seeing the results of this.'

can confirm a manager's choices.

Concerns are small expressions of doubts and fears:

> 'I'm a bit worried about the timing on this.'
> 'I'm just a bit afraid that you won't be able to get this information.'
> 'I'm concerned about the risk.'

This is no more than good communications practice. Expressions of concern, mixed with questions, are a powerful means of exploring and re-shaping risky or unwieldy contract proposals.

> 'I'm a bit worried about . . .' allows for the possibility that the proposal is perfectly achievable and the trainer is being over-anxious. But . . .
> 'The timing is wrong.'
> 'You won't get this information.'
> 'The risk's too great.'

are all very flat, unequivocal statements, with very little room for discussion. You should be very sure of your facts before you give voice to any of them.

Preferences are a form of recommendation, most often applicable when it comes to agreeing on assessment measures, when the trainer may take more of a directive role in proposing terms:

> 'I'd like to see . . .' is a better opening for a proposal for an assessment measure than
> 'You should have . . .' or
> 'We must see . . .'

Similarly,

> 'I think a good way of assessing this would be . . .'
> 'I'd prefer to see a demonstration, if possible, rather than read a report . . .'

can be honest expressions of preference.

Summary

The task of the trainer in agreeing the MLC is to use a mixture of questions and statements in order to achieve a realistic, precise and clear agreement for which the manager feels responsible.

Most of what the trainer will say should be in the form of questions: this can be difficult for trainers who are new to MLCs and more used to a directive role. Not everything a trainer says will be a question: it is necessary from time to time to provide information and advice. For the purposes of analysis we can categorise these other statements into a number of types. Where a trainer is having difficulty in negotiating effective contracts it may be because of chronic over-use or under-use of particular types of statement.

It is not possible, of course, to provide a detailed prescription for the 'correct' mixture. Negotiations vary depending on the approach and attitude of each learner/manager, and there are different styles among successful negotiators. Within the boundaries of good practice it is possible for each newcomer to develop his or her favoured style.

Support

Part of the Tutor role is to provide support to the managers who are undertaking MLCs. The support may take the form of:

- providing books or videotapes relevant to the chosen contract area.
- providing other facilities available to the training department: video playback, for example, or entry into short courses.
- providing a helpline by suggesting the manager calls if there are problems with the contract.
- telephoning or calling on the manager part-way through the MLC and asking about progress.
- organising a progress review meeting part-way through the MLC.
- organising group meetings of managers who are undertaking MLCs, to meet for mutual support.

Providing books, tapes and other facilities involves a decision about the degree of assistance and the degree of independence in an MLC (see below, Chapter 9).

A helpline is the least a trainer can offer in terms of ongoing support.

Providing support by arranging or initiating meetings during the course of an MLC has advantages and disadvantages.

- It increases the cost of the programme by using more trainer time and taking managers away from work for more time. The increased cost is on a sliding scale, of course, from the small increment of a telephone call to the expense of regular meetings.
- It makes an extra demand on trainer time, which may be in short supply quite apart from cost considerations (so a progress meeting with eight managers, lasting an hour, might be better than eight separate telephone calls).
- It provides support and motivation for some managers, who may find the individual nature of the MLC makes them feel lonely. It may make managers address hold-ups and blockages sooner rather than later, and it provides an early warning to the trainer of problems.
- It may reduce the sense of ownership and control the manager feels for the MLC, and it certainly reduces the amount of self-reliance required – which may not be a good thing.

The choice to be made here is part of the design of the programme, and different circumstances will indicate different solutions.

Box 7.13 Size and support

Decisions about support also depend on the size (and length) of the MLC. Most contracts agreed by NRMC trainers are scheduled to run over six to eight weeks. If a larger contract is proposed, it is suggested that the manager establishes assessment measures that he/she expects to meet in six to eight weeks and progress is reviewed at that point. Longer-term goals can be achieved through a number of consecutive contracts, if necessary, in keeping with MLC philosophy.

Where an MLC is agreed to run over a longer period, say for twelve weeks or for six months, it becomes more likely that the support provided by a group meeting, or by discussion with a trainer, will be valuable.

If there are to be meetings, either with the trainer or with other learners/managers, this should be indicated clearly in advance so that people can make the necessary arrangements. Some outline structure for the meetings is also desirable: e.g. each manager to give a five minute presentation to the group on the objectives of his/her contract and on progress and problems.

Assessment

If the MLC has been negotiated properly, then Assessment should not be a problem. The evidence has been specified, the criteria have been specified, or are obvious. Assessment is a time when the trainer learns about the manager's progress, and also about his/her own level of skill in negotiating effective Management Learning Contracts.

There is little to add here to what was said in the previous chapter: there we saw that the trainer's role is one of *asking questions* and *giving feedback*.

Questions are used to:

- obtain information about the manager's progress:
  'What did you do?'
  'How did you feel about that?'
  'What happened next?'

- assess the extent to which the manager has learned by evaluating what happened: 'If you were advising someone who was setting out to do what you've just done, what would you say?' 'What would you do differently next time?'

- assess the realism of any plans for the future:
  'What does this mean?'
  'When will you do this?'
  'What do you expect to achieve?'

- guide the manager's account:
  'Let's talk about the interview: what happened there?'
  'Can you tell me more about what happened before the presentation?'

Feedback includes making an assessment, congratulating, empathising with, and stretching the manager. If the contract is not satisfactory, the trainer may wish to refer or revise it, and this returns the discussion to a negotiation about what will happen next.

Training the trainers

A short training and development course for trainers who wish to use Management Learning Contracts has been developed at the Northern Regional Management Centre. It is effective in introducing trainers to the knowledge and skills necessary for implementing the MLC approach. It is no substitute for experience, but aims to complement it.

Spread over three days, with intervals of six weeks between each day, it:

- introduces the principles, aims and background of the MLC approach.
- requires each course member to devise and agree a personal learning contract, asks that it be carried out, and asks the course member to report back to the group on successes and failures. This gives most trainers an insight into the feelings of managers who undertake MLCs. (A certain proportion of trainers fail to return to report on progress, and a certain proportion of contracts fail to achieve their objectives.)
- explores detailed issues of MLC design and assessment.
- asks each course member to negotiate and assess at least two 'live' MLCs and to report on progress.

This gives trainers more confidence in their abilities, and prepares them for the challenges ahead.

In addition, trainers need to:

- establish necessary levels of expertise. It is unrealistic to expect a trainer to be expert in all possible MLC areas, but if a particular area is emerging time and again, whether it is introductory information technology or delegation skills, the trainer should learn enough about it to be able to help others.
- establish a bank of support materials. It may be appropriate for the trainer to recommend or provide a particular book, article, or videotape, to help the manager acquire the necessary knowledge base for the MLC. It is important for trainers to have the necessary knowledge to be able to point managers to sources of practical information, and for sources in much demand to be made available, perhaps by establishing a bank of materials in the training department.

The lack of this knowledge, and the lack of available materials, will make early contract negotiations more difficult and time-consuming.

Summary

In this chapter we have seen that a trainer might play a number of roles in supporting and using Management Learning Contracts: these are common roles for any training programme:

- Designer
- Organiser

- Publicist
- Recruiter
- Tutor.

In acting as a Tutor for an MLC, the trainer must be careful not to be too directive, while at the same time it is necessary to exercise some guidance over the discussion.

To do this, the trainer will ask a great many questions:

- to find out information
  - about the shape of the proposal
  - about the reasons for the proposal
  - about the initial level of learning
- to acknowledge the manager's responsibility for the contract
- to guide discussion.

It will also be necessary to provide information, through:

- Directions – in certain, limited circumstances
- Recommendations
- Setting out Options
- Summaries and Observations
- Statement about Feelings.

Part of the trainer's role is to support the manager who is undertaking the contract. We saw that there were a number of methods by which support could be provided. How it is done in any individual case should depend on decisions about:

- the need for support
- the need for individual self-reliance
- the cost and time needed to provide support.

Exercises

1. Which of the five trainer roles takes up most of your time? In which of the roles do you feel competent and experienced?

2. A manager puts forward a proposal for an MLC which seems to you to be too big, too time-consuming: what do you say?

3. A manager puts forward a proposal to: 'Develop an information system to keep track of marketing changes in your competitors' strategy.' What do you say?

4. A manager produces a detailed, typewritten MLC proposal. The learning objectives look like learning objectives, the assessment measures like assessment measures, the activities are clear and precise.

He hands it to you without a word and waits as you read through it. When you have finished reading, what do you say?

5. A manager produces a proposal that appears satisfactory in most respects, except that there is no measure of assessment against one of the learning objectives: what do you say?

Chapter 8

The training triangle

When you have completed this chapter you should be able to:

- **explain the advantages of involving the learner's boss in the negotiation and assessment of a Management Learning Contract.**
- **describe the potential dangers of this involvement.**
- **set out a strategy for making best use of the positive contribution line managers can make to the MLC process.**

Introduction

It is possible to involve a third party in the MLC process, bringing in a line manager from the learner's department to join the trainer and the learner in negotiating and assessing the MLC. This can be extremely advantageous in a number of ways, although it is not without its pitfalls. Trainers from the Northern Regional Management Centre have benefited from the inclusion of a line manager or mentor in the MLC process (and sometimes a trainer from the client's own training department). Corporate trainers, working with learners from within the company, will experience similar benefits from the assistance of the line.

The arrangement can bring together the three parties who are affected by any training and development work, but who seldom actually work together in partnership, in an explicit training triangle. This chapter explores the advantages of this arrangement, the potential problems, and how the parties can work together to make the most of the partnership.

The Ideal Role

The ideal role for the third partner is to bring to the MLC process contributions which neither the trainer nor the learner can provide. The learner's line manager should be able to make available:

- advice on training and development needs
- advice on the realism of proposals
- learning opportunities

- ongoing support
- assistance in assessment

as well as immediate recognition of the achievements of the individual learner. This wealth of provision can greatly enhance the value of any training and development and improve the relationship between line and staff.

Box 8.1 The training triangle

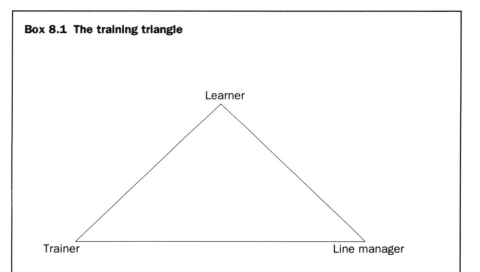

The major breakdown in communication in normal training tends to be between the trainer and the line manager, giving rise to a lack of understanding and sometimes antagonism.

Line managers (and sometimes learners) often complain about the lack of relevance of the training and the insularity of the trainers.

Trainers typically often complain about the poor motivation and negative attitudes of the line manager (and sometimes of the learners).

Learners can suffer through the ignorance of the trainers and the doubts which line managers cast on the value of the training programme.

The Management Learning Contract method can bring together these three parties in an open discussion of what the training and development should be.

(One senior training and development manager says that this results in two managers being trained for the price of one.)

Let us examine the components of this ideal role at a little more length.

Training and development needs

The assessment of training and development needs, and the initiative in proposing an MLC should come from the learner/manager, as we have seen. The advice of the line manager can be very valuable in establishing a clear picture of those needs, and a clear picture of the standards which the learner/manager should aim to achieve.

Between them, the learner and his/her boss should have a better picture of short- to middle-term development needs than anyone else, particularly in those cases when they work closely or regularly together (most often found when the learner is of junior management level) and when the development and assessment of subordinates is an explicit expectation within the company – through appraisal or succession planning schemes, for example.

Even where this degree of closeness or volume of information is not available, it can be helpful for the learner/manager to receive constructive opinions of a more senior manager about development needs.

It is the responsibility of the trainer to establish a structure for obtaining this advice, and we will explore some possibilities later in this chapter. The contribution of the line manager may operate in a range of different ways, often entailing discussion with the learner prior to a three-way discussion with the trainer, which may:

- cast doubt on a development need the learner/manager expresses and/or
- give feedback on overall strengths and needs – as seen by the line manager and/or
- recommend and promote acceptance of attention to a particular development need (but see the dangers of this, below)
- advise on the standards the learner/manager should aim to achieve.

Advice on realism

Active advice on the realism of a Management Learning Contract, particularly on the plan of action, is an invaluable contribution to the discussion of a proposal. Whereas the learner/manager may be optimistic about the ease with which he/she can gain access to information, or set up activities to progress the MLC, the line manager is likely to have a more realistic view. This of course relies upon:

Box 8.2 Standards of achievement

If the line manager is well-versed in the skill or technique the learner proposes to acquire there is no better source of advice about realistic standards of achievement, because the line manager will be familiar with the skill and the likely reactions of the environment in which it will be exercised. There will normally be grounds for the trainer to suggest additional, or amended means of assessment (such as a personal report, structured in a particular way to complement the proposals of the line manager).

If an MLC is set around an area of the Management Charter Initiative's Competence Standards, there is clear scope for discussion and agreement between the line manager and the other two parties to the contract about how the general standards apply to the specific case. The line manager is in an excellent position to help the learner and the trainer make a precise definition of the competence standard as it will apply in specific circumstances, and it will generally be appropriate to do this before the MLC is undertaken.

- greater experience of the line manager of managing people, of organisational politics and the operations of the system: this may not always apply.
- more complete knowledge of plans for the future which will affect learning opportunities; this will usually hold true.

Providing learning opportunities

The line manager may actively assist the action plan by making available learning opportunities – establishing circumstances where the learner/manager can practise a skill, or obtain certain information. This is a valuable contribution of a sort the trainer is unlikely to be able to provide.

Box 8.3 Providing an opening

The opportunity to take on a task usually performed by one's boss can lead to valuable learning. Line managers associated with NRMC programmes have delegated:

- recruitment interviews
- the presentation of reports to committees
- the lead role in representing the section/department at meetings
- leading team building exercises.

– among other things, to provide learning opportunities for individuals who have wanted to develop skills in these areas.

Ongoing support

As the MLC progresses, the learner/manager may welcome the availability of someone who will discuss progress or problems, and who shows an interest in the outcome of his/her efforts. The trainer may be a source of this support, or it may be provided by fellow learners, friends and colleagues. The line manager may be a valuable provider of support too, particularly if he/she can offer advice, or can empathise.

The line manager is best positioned, of all the learner's potential supporters, to cushion the possible harmful effects of changes in the workload, or circumstances that arise after the MLC has been agreed and threaten its successful completion, and also best positioned to allow or encourage the learner to take advantage of favourable opportunities that arise – the extra meeting to be chaired, the extra negotiation to undertake, and so on.

Assessment

We have already acknowledged that certain aspects of improved competence are difficult or impossible for a trainer or other outside assessor to evaluate. The line manager may be in a good position to:

- testify to improved performance in a range of difficult areas, from self-organisation to interpersonal skills.
- testify to the accuracy of a description or analysis provided by the learner as part of the MLC.

Overall, the line manager can play a very useful role in establishing, supporting and assessing the MLC. The benefits to the line manager are the numerous opportunities to influence the shape and form of the training and development his/her subordinates are undertaking, such that it is relevant and useful to the needs of the job. Where this is achieved, and the individual is successful, the recognition of this success by the line manager is also valuable, rewarding and motivating the individual in a way that success on closed training and development courses may fail to do.

Potential problems

For all the helpful contributions the third party can bring to the partnership there are also dangers and potential problems. These need to be recognised in order to avoid, manage or minimise them.

The absentee problem

Some line managers may simply avoid contact. They may consider training and development a waste of time. Or something that trainers and developers are paid to do. They may be extremely task-orientated and have little ability in people management. They may be extremely busy, unable to meet the trainer and the learner at a convenient time.

The action a trainer might take would depend in part on the circumstances. A clear briefing to line managers (as described below) about the extent of their role may alleviate some of the fears that lead to absenteeism. Diary dates for meetings established well in advance may cope with some of the line managers with full schedules. Some line managers are perhaps best missed out, and perhaps a substitute can be found (see the section on 'Mentors', below).

The project orientation

Line managers may be more inclined than learners to adopt a project orientation to the MLC. It can be seen as a way of getting a particular task done, or the requirements may be genuinely mistaken for a project such as the one the line manager carried out in the past, on a more traditional course of education or training.

Again the solution lies in an adequate briefing about the aims and nature of Management Learning Contracts, and the prompt use of reminders if the line manager lapses back into a project orientation during the discussions.

Short-term orientation

A focus on short-term needs – whether they are presented in project or learning contract form – may be seen as a danger of involving the line manager. This is seen most often in knowledge-biased or specific skills proposals.

Action for avoidance of this tendency, if it is expected to arise in a problematic form, may include:

- guidelines (and restrictions) on what may be chosen for an MLC.
- an emphasis on skill development, and on transferable skills, when briefing line managers.
- a systematic focus on skill development when agreeing MLCs so that some transferable element is included as well as, or instead of, part of the specific activity.

Box 8.4 Short-term benefits

Karen's line manager was new in post and determined to make changes in the operation of the department she had inherited. Her proposal for Karen's MLC was that she would analyse the time sheets for a certain section of the department and assess use of time against departmental priorities.

Quite naturally, she was supportive of this effort to the extent of releasing Karen from her normal duties for a generous amount of time each week.

She had grasped the difference between a project and a learning contract and was able to point to the information Karen would learn as the main benefit of the contract to her; while adding that she was pleased to see how a learning contract could have such relevance to the operations of the department.

As is typical is such cases the proposal was explained by the line manager, while Karen sat quietly by (see also Box 8.13 below).

Box 8.5 Restrictions

Managers undertaking the Northern Regional Management Centre's Certificate in Management Studies are required to devise one MLC (out of three) on some aspect of interpersonal skills. British Gas North Eastern, who worked in partnership with NRMC for several years to provide the programme for BGNE managers, required the learners to make the interpersonal skills MLC the *first* one of the three.

In the opinion of the trainers, both of these restrictions had beneficial effects on the programme.

- Interpersonal skills are essential to effective management, yet those least able in this area are often those least likely to propose an interpersonal skills contract.
- The restriction is not particularly confining – there are still many choices to be made.
- Managers in the BGNE scheme who tackled the IP skills contract first were more likely than managers in other organisations to continue to explore and develop interpersonal skills in their second and third contracts.

The authoritarian problem

By far the biggest potential danger in involving the line manager in the MLC process is that he/she may behave in a directive fashion and steal ownership of the MLC away from the learner/manager. Some learners in these circumstances will gratefully relinquish this troublesome responsibility, and gladly do what they're told: this is probably the nature of their natural working relationship with their boss, after all. Some learners will fight the interference, and the trainer can feel as uncomfortable in the negotiation as anyone caught in the middle of a personal argument between a married couple.

Ways of dealing with this specific problem are discussed in a separate section below. In marginal cases it can be avoided by a clear briefing to the line managers about the importance of the learner owning the MLC. At the same time, we are not asking the line manager to stand by while the learner ignores a serious need.

Box 8.6 The subordinate's contract

As we said in Chapter 5, it is possible for a learner to benefit from undertaking a contract that has been proposed by his/her boss. But only if certain conditions are met.

The MLC will only be effective if the learner:

- *accepts there is a problem:* in other words, agrees that some part of his/her job performance is not up to standard.
- *believes something can be done about it:* in other words, does not accept the present level of performance as inevitable or unchangeable.
- *is prepared to do something about it:* sees the area as a priority and is willing to concentrate on it.

If any of these three conditions does not apply, learning is very unlikely to take place (see also Box 8.14 below).

The incompetence problem

On some occasions the learner may propose an MLC in an area where the line manager is not competent. Where the line manager recognises this, the immediate danger – usually a remote one – is of unduly hurting his/her feelings or sense of self-esteem. The problem may become one of the line manager attempting to exert undue influence, as in the previous section, to steer the learner away from an area which the boss undervalues because of his/her ignorance of it.

The greater danger arises in those cases where the line manager is not competent and is unaware of this. In its extreme forms this is rare, although there may more often be an unvoiced difference of opinion between trainer and line manager as to the degree of expertise of the latter (and, of course, the same for the former). It is important for the trainer here to ensure that appropriate models and resources are supplied to the learner and that assessment does not rely on the opinion of the line manager to any extent beyond a courteous acknowledgement of that person's position (see Box 6.11).

The collusion problem

A different kind of assessment problem may arise when the line manager feels drawn closely to the learner's side of the partnership. We referred to this in Chapter 6 on Assessment.

Such an alignment can be quite natural. The two people work together and see each other on a regular basis: the trainer is just a visitor. In some cases the line manager, whatever his/her feelings about the results of the MLC, will adopt a protective stance towards the learner.

If the trainer is successful in shaping the attitudes of the line manager in the briefing prior to involvement in the MLC, some problems of collusion can be avoided, but there is no room for complacency about the success of preventive measures. Specific solutions are set out below.

The confidentiality problem

The involvement of the manager in the MLC process can introduce new information and new opportunities, but it can also be restrictive. Learners/managers do not always feel they can discuss their development needs with their boss. Sometimes this is because of the attitudes of the boss. Sometimes because of the particular need in question. (It is not unusual, for example, for a learner to analyse his/her time management problem and find that a major cause of it is the boss.)

A learner may be restricted, or feel unwilling to express a particular development need because of the role designed for the line manager in the MLC process. This is truly a cost of the line manager's involvement. It may be justified by reference to the many good MLCs agreed with the help of line managers. Any hardship it causes may be eased by creating opportunities for the restricted individual to discuss his/her problem with the trainer or with fellow learners. A chosen mentor might even be used, as part of the design of the scheme, to avoid such a cost being incurred.

There is little point in engaging line managers of learners in negotiating and assessing Management Learning Contracts without being aware of the possible problems. It should be clear from the diverse nature of the problem factors that they are unlikely all to be present in the same individual.

Box 8.7 Problem types

The three most common problem types are:

1. **The nurturing type**: protective and parental, this type can help a manager to develop by giving helpful advice on apparent needs and making opportunities available. The danger is that there may be a reluctance to let go and allow the learner to make independent decisions. In the shorter term, the immediate problem may lie in a protective attitude towards the learner when the MLC is assessed, and the trainer needs to be wary of the opinions and the expressions of satisfaction of the nuturing type. In addition to their natural instincts of protection, they may have become so involved in initiating and shaping the contract that they feel a sense of ownership for it, and this inclines them to be lenient in their assessments.

2. **The directive type**: typically orientated towards the task, the project and the needs of the department, this type does not encourage a learner to explore and discuss skill-developments, and needs to be discouraged from seeking short-term benefits on every occasion.

3. **The empty chair**: this type is often absent from discussions, whether physically or only mentally. He/she creates problems by providing little or no support or enlightening information. This type will often be lenient in any contribution to assessment, perhaps because this is the line of least resistance.

There is a fourth type who may create problems for the trainer: *The expert*, who may wish to debate the trainer's methods, or propose particular prescriptive approaches to learning areas. By no means common, the expert can combine an argumentative approach to the trainer with an approach to the learner that is both directive and nurturing. There is tendency to be critical at assessment.

When encountering the expert, it is good practice to be particularly careful to avoid the learner being crushed in any trainer–line manager arguments.

Some of the dangers can be avoided, or their effects minimised by a careful pre-briefing, and some can be combated in the negotiations and assessments themselves. We will consider how to do this in the last part of this chapter. Before that, we should consider an alternative to the line manager. Why not use a mentor system instead?

Mentors

In this context, a mentor is a manager other than the learner's boss, who is charged with advising and counselling the learner, and is drawn into the Management Learning Contract process as a third partner.

Where mentors are used – in this context or as part of a more generalised helping relationship – they tend to be senior to the learner, although not necessarily senior in the same line or department.

There are strengths and weaknesses in using mentors in the MLC partnership rather than the learner's boss.

On the positive side we might expect:

- mentors will be more sympathetic to a learning/development approach to the MLC and less project-orientated, simply because they will not have the dual motives of even the best of managers, divided between the desire to develop their subordinates and the need to get work out of them.
- mentors should be more sympathetic to a learning/development approach if they have volunteered for the role, or carried it out in the past, or are mentors for several people (see Box 8.8). This does not reduce the need for clear guidance as to their role in the partnership, of course.
- mentors are less likely to be too directive or to collude with the learner over the assessment.
- the problems of confidentiality may not arise in the same form as when the third partner is the learner's boss, but much depends on the relationship between the mentor and the boss, and the degree of trust between mentor and the learner.

Box 8.8 Recruiting mentors

Much of what is said here assumes that mentors are willing volunteers, naturally interested in developing others, who are able to find the necessary time to discuss matters with their charges, and become skilled at their role by virtue of experience. The use of the word 'mentor' is not a magic spell, however, which transforms management styles or approaches.

C and E Ltd, an engineering company, decided on a mentoring system to support ten young middle managers through a development programme which included workshops and Management Learning Contracts. The mentors were appointed by a senior management group. The company culture was very task-orientated and this was reflected in the approach of the 'mentors' who either became involved with the learners in a directive, authoritarian fashion, or took no initiatives to contact their charges at all.

On the negative side, however, we are likely to find:

- less of an ability to cast independent light on the learner's development needs. (Of course the line manager's opinions on this matter can be sought outside the mentor–learner relationship.)

- less of an ability to advise on the realism of the MLC, or to assist the action plan by making learning opportunities available.
- less of an ability to assist in assessment through witness testimony or through validating the accuracy of technical information. (Of course, this testimony can still be sought from the line manager if required.)

In considering both the positive and negative features of a mentor system, we have been dealing with possibilities and likelihoods, rather than certainties, because much of the effectiveness of the role depends upon the personalities and skills of the individuals involved. A manager who acts as a mentor on a number of occasions, with different people, is likely to develop more skill in the role of the Third Partner, but a sensitive and intelligent line manager is more closely linked to the realities of the learner's job performance: the real world of managerial work. Because of this linkage, the line manager is always part of the Training Triangle, whether or not he/she is one of the parties to the MLC, because the judgements and decisions that most affect the learner's job are made at that point (see Box 8.9).

The choice about whether to involve line managers or mentors will be made on the circumstances of each company's case. For the remainder of this chapter we will refer to the third partner as the line manager or the boss of the learner, simply for convenience, while recognising that much of what is said applies equally well if a mentor is filling the role.

Making the most of the partnership

Certain simple measures can go a long way towards making the most of the contribution the third partner can bring to the MLC process.

First and foremost, a clear pre-briefing, explaining what is about to happen and the line manager's role in making it happen successfully.

Secondly, preparation against the common difficulties, to limit the damage they can do. These measures will not solve all the problems all the time but they will make the trainer's life easier and the Management Learning Contracts more effective.

Pre-briefing

What is called for is similar to the Priming process for learners/managers, that:

Box 8.9 The extended training triangle

The strong relationship between the implicit criteria we use to evaluate training and development, and job performance (and its natural assessor, the boss) means that the boss will usually remain a part of the geometry.

Where a mentor is used, he/she should be seen as forming a separate relationship and is not simply substituting for the boss:

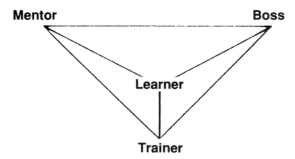

Rather than one triangle – or three-way meeting – there are now four possible three-way discussions of the learner's progress.

Even if the boss takes no active part in agreeing the MLC, and does not discuss the matter at all with mentor or trainer, there will usually be a relationship with the learner which adds to the latter's perceptions of what he/she should do, and which includes an assessment by the line manager, of the effects of the training and development.

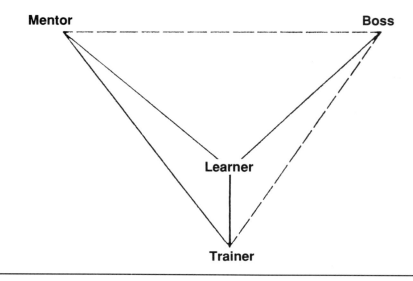

- explains the MLC approach.
- builds motivation and confidence in it.
- explains the line manager's role.

Ideally this pre-briefing will take place at about the same time as the learners are being primed. As with the learners, the line managers should be briefed face-to-face: printed materials might be used to support the briefing, but they will be insufficient in themselves. Experience indicates that the learners will not brief their line managers effectively, so this must be done by the trainer.

The explanation of the MLC method will be the same explanation as that provided to the learners, and the same measures should be taken to build confidence in it. The rest of the briefing has a different slant, however, to the Priming, and where possible it is more effective to speak to the line managers separately. This means that throughout the explanation of the MLC it is explicit that this is a process the learner will be going through, and the choices and flexibility and responsibility are those of the learner, not the line manager.

It is important to explain and to stress three key features of the MLC method, in order to try to avoid problems later on:

- *A Management Learning Contract is not the same as a project:* it is about learning and developing skills, not just about doing things
- *The payback to the line manager and to the company is not immediate.* The Management Learning Contract should be relevant to the job and should fit in with current work performance, but line managers should not expect an instant return.
- *The MLC works best if the initiative comes from the individual learner* and he/she feels responsible for the proposal. The line manager has a role to play in providing help and advice – and some home truths might be called for at times – but, like the trainer, he/she must be careful not to threaten the learner's sense of responsibility for the proposal.

These three points need to be made in a friendly but uncompromising way. They are fundamental rules: they are not open to negotiation. It is quite natural for line managers to forget these principles or by their behaviour to ignore them later on, so it is very important for the trainer to set them out clearly at an early stage, so that those who later transgress can be reminded of them.

As with the learners/managers, the line managers should be given a clear idea of their role (see Box 8.10), setting out what is expected of them, how long it will take, when it is scheduled.

Box 8.10 What is required

Like the learners, the line managers will have certain practical questions about the process. They will want to know about:

- the subject of the MLC: How is it chosen? Are there restrictions on the freedom of choice?
- the timing: the scheduling and the size of the MLC.
- assessment: How will the MLC be assessed? Who will carry out the assessment?

The role of the line manager can be broken down into:

- *Pre-contract discussions:* assisting the learner with diagnosis of his/her development needs.
- *Agreeing the MLC:* ideally by attending a meeting with the learner and trainer.
- *Supporting progress:* What form this takes will depend upon the actual MLC – it may involve little more than taking an interest in how the learner is getting on, or the contract may involve working closely with the learner.
- *Assessment:* again, attendance of a meeting with the learner and the trainer is ideal.

An explanation of the details of what is asked of line managers at each of these four stages under your particular scheme will be helpful. It is also helpful to stress that the role is quite simple – as opposed to being complex or difficult – and not particularly time-consuming, but of great potential value to the learner. This addresses two of the line manager's principal fears and provides an additional reason why he/she should get involved.

Handling problems

The pre-briefing will avoid some of the problems we have discussed in this chapter, but it will not avoid all of them all of the time. As the trainer you will need to cope with them as they arise in the negotiation.

1. Problem

The line manager puts forward or supports a project. (This will often be accompanied by a large amount of 'background' setting out recent and anticipated developments in the department and will frequently lead to a project of acquiring or analysing information or establishing a new information system.)

Action: immediate

Look for the learning, or ask the line manager and the learner to look. Remind them of the rules.

Words

'This sounds to me like a project: it's about producing something. What are you actually going to learn?' (addressed to the learner/manager).

Action: follow up

If possible, you might button-hole the line manager for a chat after the three-way discussion.

Words

'Where do you see Frank going with future contracts?'
'What kind of skills does he need to work on?'
'What does he think about it?'

Box 8.11 A little bit less, a little bit more

Jack, who was Clive's line manager, wanted the contract to be about preparing a set of clear statements about company policy and procedures in respect of certain personnel practices. The policy at the commencement of the contract was to be found in the original legislation and in a variety of union–management agreements and statements by management committees. Jack and Clive worked in the personnel section of one of the company's large departments: whenever a query arose about policy or procedure, Clive had to respond personally. Jack wanted Clive to create a set of guidance notes, written in plain English, explaining policy and procedures in the common problem areas, to reduce the number of queries.

Clive agreed that this would be a sensible measure.

The proposal was, of course, a project: after some discussion the principal learning area (clear written expression) was identified.

Jack wanted Clive to produce guidance notes in twenty different areas by the end of the contract period. These were the main areas Jack had identified as giving rise to queries (at the head of the list, for example, was the procedure for arranging for maternity leave).

The trainer said that production of notes in all twenty areas was not necessary for completion of the MLC: he suggested a sample of notes from three areas.

The notes themselves, however, would not be sufficient to complete the contract. The trainer suggested some reflection on and evaluation of the ways in which Clive had taken the complex statements of his sources and turned them into simple, clear points that the average employee could understand.

Changing the line manager's project proposals into effective MLCs will often involve this twin process: reducing the output requirement and increasing the amount of other kinds of evidence required, to focus on learning.

This action may jog the line manager onto the true MLC path – or it may alert you to the likelihood that all future negotiations will involve a struggle with someone who doesn't see the idea.

Box 8.12 Without moving your lips

The clearest sign of this is when the line manager explains what the contract proposal is about.

The trainer might greet the learner and line manager, and after the initial pleasantries ask the learner, 'Have you decided what you want to do?'

'We think the contract should be about . . .' a voice replies, but it is not the learner's voice.

Where the direction has all taken place before the meeting, and the line manager is more of the nurturing than the straightforward directive type (see Box 8.7, above) the learner might give the initial reply, with sideways glances to the line manager. If the learner has difficulty with the explanation the line manager will quickly come to the rescue and explain the proposal, which has probably originated with him/her in any case.

---

2. Problem
The line manager is directive and puts forward the MLC proposal.

Action
Check out the acceptance of the proposal with the individual learner.

Box 8.13 Group support

An effective – although time-consuming – method of supporting learners and line managers who face dilemmas in this area is to set up separate support groups for each, so that learners meet regularly as a group and line managers who are involved in agreeing and assessing contracts also meet on a regular (although probably less frequent) basis.

In a group setting, learners are more likely to be forthcoming about whether they or their manager came up with the initial proposal for the MLC, and about whether they feel they are really exercising choice.

Similarly, if a number of line managers are successfully working within the MLC system as intended, and are seeing positive results from it (which should be the case) then their experiences, shared in discussion, are more likely to have a positive effect on the future behaviour of 'problem' line managers than a one-to-one discussion with a trainer.

Although this method is time consuming, it can be more efficient than attempting to sort out a number of problems through one-to-one meetings.

If it is to be used, line managers and learners need to be told about it in good time, and dates fixed for meetings. The atmosphere suffers if the meetings are called hurriedly, for remedial or emergency repair reasons.

Words

'How do you feel about this, Frank?'
'Do you see a need for this?'

This may have only a limited effect, but at least it acknowledges the consent of the learner/manager. Any further measures involve separate discussions with one or both of the other parties.

3. Problem

The line manager and the learner have different ideas about what the learner/manager should do, and this results in conflict.

Action

If the conflict is apparent in the three-way discussion, you may play a mediating role, helping each party clarify what they propose and exploring underlying reasons for the proposals and the difference of opinion.

Such open conflict is not usual. More often the disagreements will have been worked out between the learner and the line manager before they meet the trainer, although sometimes the trainer is drawn into the dispute by one party or another (see Box 8.14).

4. Problem

The line manager appears very protective of the learner when it comes to assessment of the MLC.

Action and words: immediate

It can be best to welcome and explore the contribution the line manager is able to provide by asking for more information: if he/she says that the learner's time management has improved then you might ask for details – What specific things have happened to indicate improvement? How many examples of improved performance can he/she cite?

A way of turning the questions back to the learner is to begin by asking about how he/she feels:

'Well, we've just heard that your boss thinks you're doing a much better job of organising your time: How do you feel about that?' And the follow-up questions are about what the learner has done or has thought.

Alternatively, the questions can be turned back to the learner by referring to a specific point in any report or written material he/she has provided.

Where you consider that the MLC has been completed, but some constructive criticism is called for, in order to inform or to stretch the

---

Box 8.14 The reluctant learner

Clark was enrolled on a Management Development Programme involving MLCs and made poor progress. He missed deadlines, produced sub-standard work, argued with his assessors and with his fellow learners, and produced a succession of bizarre reasons to excuse his poor performance. His first Management Learning Contract was eventually completed to the letter of the agreement, but both the line manager and the trainer were concerned about the lack of evaluation by Clark of what he had done, and about the extent to which the results had fallen short of the spirit of the original intent.

Clark's line manager asked for a separate meeting with the trainer and asked for advice. Clark was a poor manager, he said, who had difficulty producing consistent results and who caused tension and disruption in the section team; he ignored advice about how he should improve, and generally insisted that everything was going well, or if not, then it was the fault of someone else. What Clark needed, the line manager said, was something to make him open his eyes and take an honest look at himself.

Clark did not take the initiative in proposing a contract area (maintaining that it was hard to see what he could improve upon). The trainer suggested that, as he had evidently had trouble managing his learning (his slow progress and difficulties with the Management Development Programme were a matter of record) he might consider examining his approach to learning again. He had already completed a Learning Styles Questionnaire at the beginning of the programme: Why didn't he do that again? And, to provide more information, from a number of perspectives, why not ask four or five other people who worked with him to complete one for him? Clark agreed to do this, and the feedback began to open up some of the discrepancies between how he saw his behaviour and how others saw it.

In this case, the reasons of the line manager appeared genuine and the 'learner' appeared to be avoiding the processes of self-examination necessary for genuine learning. Where entry onto the development programme is voluntary, such individuals are, fortunately, rare.

---

learner, it is important to avoid an over-protective reaction from the line manager, by reaching explicit agreement that the MLC is complete before summarising and presenting your criticisms.

Undoubtedly the greatest difficulty arises when the disagreement is such that you do not accept that the MLC has been completed, but the line manager says that everything is satisfactory. This is a very rare occurrence; the nature of the written agreement will usually guard against it.

Action: in future.

If on one occasion the protective attitude of the line manager has created a sense of unease about the value of his/her opinions, you should aim in future contracts to:

- specify more precisely what the line manager will assess, and how
- specify additional assessment measures (see Box 8.15).

Box 8.15 The scope of discretion

On a time management contract it is not unusual to look for some testimony from the line manager as to the effect of the MLC. An assessment measure might be:

'A statement from the line manager testifying to improved self-organisation over the period of the MLC'.

This gives room for opinion, but the trainer can always ask for examples and for the evidence on which the opinion is based.

A more controlled approach to this assessment would be to agree that the line manager would make a suitable witness and then to discuss criteria, and to formulate an assessment measure that might read:

'The line manager to testify whether:
(a) requests for information are dealt with promptly.
(b) the learner's desk and in-tray are organised and tidy.
(c) adequate warning of any changes known to the learner is passed on promptly to the line manager'.

And so on. It is generally best to keep the points to a small, manageable number, but require the line manager to relate any opinions to agreed and observable indications of performance.

Conclusions

The partnership of the Training Triangle can be very effective in establishing and assessing relevant and practical Management Learning Contracts. The line manager of the learner has a distinct and valuable role to play. The actual value of the line manager's contribution will depend in part on the attitudes and skills of the particular individual, and in part on the skills of the trainer in providing an adequate and timely briefing and in dealing with predictable problems as they arise.

Summary

In this chapter we considered the benefits and the risks of involving the learner's line manager in agreeing and assessing the MLC.

The line manager is able to:

- advise on the learner's training and development needs
- advise on the practicality of proposals
- create learning opportunities in the work-place
- provide ongoing support and counselling
- assist in assessing the MLC

Involving the line manager is not without problems or risks. The learner's boss may be:

- too concerned with projects or with short-term needs
- too directive
- too protective
- not competent to help the learner
- not interested in helping the learner.

And when the line manager is involved, the learner may not wish to discuss or to tackle certain problems because of concerns about confidentiality.

It may be in particular cases that the costs appear to outweigh the benefits and rather than use line managers, the involvement of other managers, to act as mentors, is sought.

Generally, mentors may be more positive in attitude and more skilled than line managers, although much depends on the individual, but line managers will always be involved – explicity or implicitly – in the training by virtue of their position.

Finally we saw that the trainer can help to make the most of the partnership, whether it involves a line manager or a mentor, by:

- pre-briefing and preparing the third partner
- being prepared to tackle common problems when they arise.

Exercise

1. What kind of contribution might a line manager make to the discussion of an MLC proposal on:
    (a) Learning computer skills?
    (b) Learning financial analysis techniques?

2. Some of the potential problems of involving line managers in the MLC process are:
    - they may be too directive and/or too protective
    - they avoid involvement and give no support
    - they are too project-orientated.

    In your experience, why might they behave in these ways?

3. In priming the individual learner to prepare for using an MLC we saw how we might motivate him/her. How might you motivate a line manager?

Part Three

Range and scope of MLCs

by David Thompson

Chapter 9

Range and scope of MLCs

When you have completed this chapter you should be able to:

- **identify four different perspectives in approaching MLCs.**
- **identify how MLCs can be comparable in terms of stretch, size and quality.**
- **understand how growth in a learner/manager is affected by internal and external factors.**
- **identify strategies for increasing growth in a learner/manager.**
- **recognise the range of opportunities for growth that are available.**

In Chapter 5, we looked at the principles for negotiating a successful MLC. It is important to recognise that the MLC is not a mechanistic approach to learning. In fact it is impossible for a mechanistic approach to succeed, given all the variables of different learners, different approaches to learning, different opportunities.

The trainer therefore needs a range of 'structures' or 'perspectives' to help manage all the variables.

Staged development

One of the key principles of MLCs is that learning should be an incremental or 'staged' process. This implies that there are clear steps to be taken up a ladder of development, and that the size and number of steps are only limited by the 'resources' available.

Box 9.1 shows a simple model of staged development for interviewing skills where at the bottom end the requirement is to identify the principles of good practice and to 'have a go' in order for the learning manager to assess more accurately his or her own standards of ability. At the higher end, the learner/manager is an experienced interviewer but has identified a problem that needs resolving and has to learn specific skills to overcome that problem. One can assume that the ladder never really ends, or at least ends only at a stage where competence matches the requirements of the job and of the environment.

This model is helpful in that it encourages the learner/manager to view the development of learning as a series of manageable 'chunks'.

Box 9.1 Staged development

Management Learning Contracts set short-term, achievable learning objectives. To do this the learner has to have a view of what the next step is up their particular 'ladder' of skills development. This 'ladder' applies to interviewing skills, but the model could apply to any skill. No two ladders will be the same.

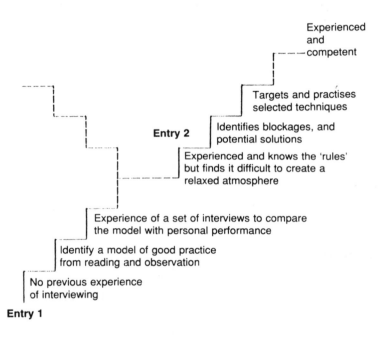

Experienced
and
— — —competent

Targets and practises
selected techniques

Entry 2

Identifies blockages, and
potential solutions

Experienced and knows the 'rules'
but finds it difficult to create a
relaxed atmosphere

Experience of a set of interviews to compare
the model with personal performance

Identify a model of good practice
from reading and observation

No previous experience
of interviewing

Entry 1

It is usual, though not a necessity, for a person at the bottom of the ladder to acquire a sound knowledge base on which to start building. At any step, however, a statement of knowledge will be required in a Management Learning Contract whether as a statement of current needs, the identification of new techniques or perspective, or as a statement concluding what has been learnt.

It is helpful to the trainer as well in that it enables some comparison to be made between contracts of different levels. One can equate 'stretch' or the degree of movement. The risk for the inexperienced trainer is that the series of steps to be taken in any one skill area becomes fixed in a general pattern or becomes too large. The exact nature of the next step for any learner/manager and their approach to it is in fact determined by the resources available specifically to them.

A simple concept that enhances the idea of staged development is of moving up through four stages.

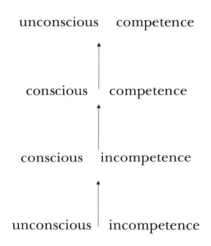

unconscious   competence

conscious   competence

conscious   incompetence

unconscious   incompetence

To begin with, the learner/manager has to identify where his or her needs are, then to practise skills consciously to the extent that they become second nature. One would expect though at the unconscious competence stage, the learner/manager should continue to appraise his or her own performance, to be able on reflection to articulate and explain the reasoning behind any course of action.

Depth and breadth

MLCs can be situated anywhere on the continuum of development from low level to high level. According to need they can also be broader or narrower in focus. It is worth having a visual picture of 'short and fat' and 'tall and thin' approaches to a learning topic. There are of course many variations within. With this in mind it is possible to compare one MLC to another in terms of volume.

In Box 9.2 skill is seen as having two dimensions, depth and breadth, that is the range of situations in which that skill is required. There are no real limits to the skill. If the model is applied to the skill

Box 9.2 Depth and breadth

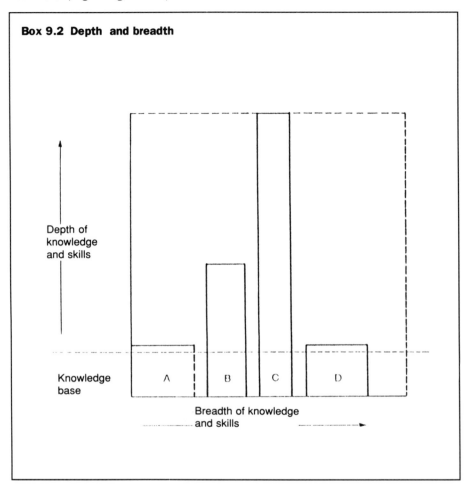

of chairing meetings then four different sets of knowledge and skill could be:

Contract A

Essentially knowledge based, identifying a framework of good practice, and assessing performance against the framework.

Contract B

Chairing a particular type of meeting, for example a committee meeting, where the knowledge base is slightly narrower and more emphasis is put on improving practice.

Contract C

A specific skill needs to be developed in chairing meetings, for example gaining commitment from others, where the knowledge base is narrower still but where a high degree of performance could be expected.

Contract D

Again essentially a knowledge based contract but at a higher level, for example where an understanding of issues related to the board of directors is required.

Management cycle

One of the best known models for describing any management activity is the Management Cycle. The activity of managing is broken down into planning, organising, motivating, controlling, with each of these activities being bonded together by communication and co-ordination (*NRMC 1990*). Structured Learning is a management activity, and using the Management Cycle can help the trainer ensure the scope of activities undertaken by the learner/manager is sound.

This is particularly important when it comes to researching and gathering information. Learner/managers more often than not have limited experience in doing this, and what they do is usually haphazard.

Planning
- What information is needed to achieve the learning objective and what are the sources?
- How much and of what sort?
- How will the learner/manager know the information he/she is getting is the right information?

Organising
- Scheduling a timetable to gather information.
- Ensuring the information is available at the right time.

Motivating
- Getting the boss to give some time off to get the information.
- Get people to give information in the format the learner/manager wants and at the right time.

Controlling
- Testing the information, and cross-checking if necessary.

- Evaluating the information against previous experience or other credible sources of ideas.

Good co-ordination and communication by the learner/manager in those four activities will ensure learning is structured and has a better chance of being more effective.

Growth opportunities and constraints

Box 9.3 gives a model of the learner/manager attempting to 'grow' outwards. The amount of 'stretch' or movement achieved in an MLC is governed by the 'resources' available. The 'resources' are not just the conventional ones of books, videos, etc. but include all factors where the lack or limitation of them prevents learning. Identifying these factors will help determine the best approach to an MLC. The structure of an MLC is also governed by the 'resources' available.

Motivation

All the evidence confirms that the principle of ownership is a major determinant in ensuring the success of an MLC. That said, however, the learner/manager must have a desire to improve. Chapter 5 looked at strategies a trainer can use during the negotiation phase of an MLC for a learner/manager who does not perceive any need to improve. Even where a learner/manager does express a desire to improve, the motivation to invest the necessary effort may not really exist.

Experience suggests there are two motivational issues to be considered:

- Does the learner/manager see the benefits of the learning outweighing the costs of having to 'work' at learning?
- Who will reward the learner/manager for succeeding in achieving the learning objectives, or who will punish for failure?

Ideally, benefits outweighing the costs in combination with praise or increased responsibility from the boss and a sense of personal satisfaction in completing a challenge will motivate the learner/manager. Successful contracts have been done, however, if the learner/manager's personal drive outweighs the indifference of the boss and, on the other hand, where the company insists on the achievement of a formal qualification as a prerequisite for promotion (see Box 4.2).

Box 9.3 Learner/manager 'resources'

Learning style

Job requirements

Learning ability

Organisation
requirements

Accurate
assessment of
current abilities

Time

**Current level of
performance**

Access
sources of
knowledge

Motivation

Measure of
competence

Desired level
of performance

Organisation requirements

The trainer has to be careful with MLCs that go into potentially
sensitive areas. Some learning topics may even be taboo in some
organisations and it is essential that the manager's boss confirms the
topic is acceptable. The experienced trainer will also have a feel for

the organisational culture and should be in a position to ask questions to check acceptability.

With most sensitive topics, however, the approach can be adjusted to allow for successful learning.

Box 9.4 The 'politically unacceptable' contract

Susan worked for a local authority where performance appraisal was not part of the formal agreement between management and unions. At the negotiation of the MLC, Susan initially wished to 'introduce an appraisal system within her department'. Her boss said this would be unacceptable, certainly in any formal sense. The MLC eventually concentrated on acquiring appraisal skills in an informal setting, i.e. how to give criticism, how to set targets in tasks and behaviours, how to coach, etc. In fact, the word 'appraisal' never featured in her series of informal 'interviews' with her team.

Job requirements

Many people work to job descriptions. These rarely give a full picture of what is required to carry out the job successfully. Sometimes they can become barriers, whether real or perceived, to personal development. This is particularly so in organisational cultures which are more task oriented, or driven by procedures.

Box 9.5 The inhibited manager

Peter worked as a unit assembly manager in a greenfield factory. It was considered by outsiders in more established local companies as setting standards for efficiency, quality and control systems. Peter was given targets on a monthly basis and given the autonomy to organise and control resources to meet them. At his first contract negotiation he said he had a problem getting material from the supplies department. The training officer for the company (the line manager was not present) suggested that Peter could consider improving relationships with the supplies department and 'networking' skills would be a useful learning topic. Peter replied that he couldn't justify being away from the shop floor. It transpired that he perceived his boss 'rewarded' or 'punished' him solely on the basis of units through the door, and that achieving outputs could only be done if he was present on the shop floor. In other words, he felt he needed to be seen to be working at all times. The MLC goal remained as networking skills, but the approach included developing a closer working relationship with the boss, away from the shop floor.

Learning abilities

Some people learn faster than others; that means that in any given time period they can learn more. Some people have illusions about being able to do something and do not realise the amount of learning that has to be done first. It is important for the trainer not to allow the learner/manager to overburden him or herself. It is easy to say that one will read 'two or three books' on a subject, or that one will 'prepare and distribute a questionnaire to assess attitudes' on a particular matter – but actually carrying out these things is more difficult and more time consuming.

It can sometimes come as a pleasant surprise when a person's learning ability is greater than expected. This is often the case with the learner/manager who has been carrying out his or her job without any real thought who, by doing an MLC, becomes 'switched on'.

Box 9.6 The 'switch on'

Les was keen to 'improve the morale of the shop' and wanted to 'learn about motivation'. During the discussion at the MLC negotiation Les showed no understanding of motivation and his role in it, and showed no critical analysis ability. This led the trainer to feel Les's learning ability was limited. Eventually the learning objective became crystallised as 'To learn how I motivate/demotivate people by observing what I say and do'. Essentially this was a process of keeping a detailed log. At the end of the contract, Les had not only identified a good range of motivators/demotivators in his behaviour with others but was questioning his whole approach to the job. This 'inner' growth was so substantial and his desire to question, listen and think things through so evident that his colleagues began to think of him as a new person.

Time

More or less time spent on an MLC will affect the quality of learning. It is not unreasonable to agree a target of how far a learner/manager can go by first asking how much time is available to the requirements of learning. The issue here for a successful MLC is to separate out what learning can be done through normal work activities and what learning has to be done as 'study' outside of normal work activities. At the minimum, some preparation and some reflection on what has been learned are likely to be contract activities that take place outside of the scope of the normal job role. At the maximum, the contract could consist entirely of activities the learner would not be likely to undertake at all in normal circumstances. More often, a blend is achieved of 'normal job' and contract activities. Few managers who are prepared to tackle an MLC are not prepared to do some 'overtime'.

Accurate assessment of current abilities

Chapter 4 looked at strategies of diagnosing learning needs. These will help reduce the problems often incurred by the inexperienced trainer who blithely assumes a person knows him or herself well enough to make an initial accurate self-assessment. Nevertheless, identifying the start point for an MLC, particularly in soft skill areas, can still be problematical. In these cases, it is reasonable to make the very purpose of the MLC an audit of personal ability.

Box 9.7 The contract as an audit

Harry was a computer manager who serviced the computing needs of a small local authority. He began by saying he felt he wanted to improve relationships with his 'customers'. He was able to describe situations reasonably well but wasn't able to come to solid conclusions as to what to do better. From the trainer's point of view he was a 'difficult' learner/manager as he was very hard to pin down. Eventually, out of frustration, the trainer offered Harry the idea of role-set analysis whereby Harry could 'identify the purpose and mutual expectations of all the people he dealt with'. Harry was taken with the idea once a structured approach had been explained. For assessment, he was to produce a 'map' of relationships showing purpose and mutual expectations. From this, he was to produce a detailed action plan of what improvements or alterations he would make, and what skills and knowledge he would need to make the changes. The MLC had become a diagnosis, with the action plan as a clear statement of the current level of ability.

Measure of competence

Here, all that needs to be said with reference to the range and scope of a contract that leads to competence is to ask the learner/manager 'If that is the level of performance required of you, what skills and knowledge do you need to acquire to get there?' Starting from the end point of 'competence' and looking back, you may see one, two or more learning steps that need to be taken (see Box 9.8).

Learning styles

The learning cycle is either explicitly or implicitly part of any MLC. The trainer should be able to identify each stage. The only possible

---

Box 9.8 Steps to competence

Joan, an employee relations officer, had been promoted to Personnel Manager with the additional responsibility for training. She was asked to put forward a comprehensive training policy proposal to meet the organisation's requirements for the next five years. While there were no formal 'competence statements' for doing this, her bosses obviously expected her to do this competently.

Knowing the 'output' or end point, she looked backwards to identify what she had to learn to achieve it. In the end she did three MLCs. First an MLC that concentrated on information gathering on training issues, both inside and outside the organisation. Secondly an MLC that concentrated on assessing the practical requirements of the various departments by discussing matters of detail with colleagues. And thirdly, as she felt her ideas were radical, an MLC on determining the impact of change and likely causes of resistance so that her proposals would, in her words, 'pre-empt any negative reaction'.

---

omission may be 'action' if an MLC concentrates on acquiring a knowledge base. With any skills development 'action' must be included. The main issues here that affect the approach to a contract are

- where on the learning cycle will the learner/manager enter the MLC?

- which aspects of the learning cycle are given emphasis according to the preferred learning styles?

Differing learning styles can be accommodated within different MLCs. Reflector-Theorists are more likely to feel comfortable doing background reading and keeping logs, while Pragmatist-Activists will want to learn new techniques and to put them into action. The contract negotiator must use his or her judgement as to whether to encourage aspects of less-preferred learning styles (see Box 9.9). Not all learner/managers are keen to keep 'logs' or personal development journals!

Sources of knowledge

Knowledge provides the sound underpinning for skills and competence development. Within an MLC, the sources of knowledge are potentially very varied. The trainer must help the learner/manager identify what these sources might be in practice and agree a strategy suitable to the learner/manager's learning style.

Box 9.9 Learning styles

Richard had done well on his first contract, interviewing and selecting a supervisor for his team. He had looked for a model of good practice and the required evidence of the job specification, structured question checklist and notes on each candidate with a rationale for why one person was chosen. At assessment time however, his line manager commented that he had received a complaint from the Personnel Department that Richard had used a personality probing questionnaire of questionable validity, 'borrowed' from a friend who had had a one day training course and who said it 'worked'. Richard became very defensive when questioned on this.

In a subsequent contract, Richard's objective was to develop team building skills to improve a small project he was running. He had heard of Belbin and was keen to try out his ideas. To focus attention on the possibilities of improving the quality of his learning by developing his Reflector-Theorist learning styles, the contract negotiator suggested Richard could not only read the book outlining Belbin's theories but also spend the first part of the contract observing in detail interactions within other teams in order to reach 'better' conclusions and to draw up a 'better' actions plan for implementing his new found ideas. Richard agreed and kept a log of behaviours observed and conclusions reached for three weeks. Once he saw the benefits arising, the Pragmatist streak in him quickly approved.

Susan's first contract was to learn skills in designing some publicity material for a project she was managing. She was very keen to 'get it right', so keen in fact that after every new idea learnt from books or other people she altered the specification and missed the deadline. While she had met the contract requirements, and met them well, inevitably her line manager was not pleased.

Her second contract was to learn 'enough' about the company accounting procedures in order to draw up her department's budget for the year. She agreed as her first activity to visit with her line manager the head of finance in order to draw up a detailed action plan or rather, a personal training plan, of what background reading she would do, who she would see, what specific information she would. need and when. While this may seem overly structured in approach, the success of getting the job done satisfactorily this time led her to realise that setting limitations, either self-imposed or imposed by others was essential.

Susan continued to be a perfectionist but she had at least learnt to balance perfectionism with pragmatism by asking 'What are the standards I have to reach in terms of quality, cost and time?

- *Books* – prescriptive. Bookshelves groan with 'How to . . .' books. They can be useful in providing checklists, tips and simple techniques, often in a simple and easy to read format. For many managers, especially pragmatists and activists, this is all they need to 'go out and do'. Inevitably though, they have their limitations; without adequate reflection, the knowledge base may be superficial.

– descriptive. Ex-captains of industry tend to write these, but so do current practitioners. Within MLCs they are best used as case studies from which the learner/manager can establish his/her own conclusions.

Experienced trainers will know which books provide the best sources of ideas. One risk is that the trainer may prescribe his or her own preferred sources (see 'Interventions' below). Another risk is that the learner/manager becomes over-burdened with reading.

- **Videos** – commercial. As with books, the experienced trainer will know which ones have most to offer the learner/manager. Their use within MLCs is best seen as providing a 'model' of practice similar to prescriptive type books. Their use of visual examples though can provide a deeper insight.
  – self-made. The development of interpersonal skills such as presentations can benefit from the learner/manager observing his or her own performance. The learner/manager will still need to have identified a model of good practice beforehand in order to know what to look for, so self-made videos can best be described as aiding reflection in order to enhance the knowledge base.

- **Observation** As an activity within an MLC, this is similar to self-made videos, but obviously allows the learner/manager to watch other people. Again, this is best done when the learner/manager knows what to look for, in order to test theory against practice (see Box 9.10).

- **Instruction** Where a learner/manager wishes to learn and apply a company procedure, this is best done by finding out what the rules and regulations are. Learning selection skills, for example, may involve generic skills being adapted to fit in with organisational procedures.

- **Advice** Finding out what others do, inside or outside the organisation, by talking through events is a powerful source of knowledge. It has the added benefit of developing closer relationships with people who might not otherwise have been approached.

- **Reflection** All MLCs require a degree of reflection.
  There are three strategies:

Box 9.10 Reflection models

Reflection Model I

Many learner/managers find it difficult to structure their analysis of events. The simplest way identifies behaviours of 'doing, saying and feeling:

(1)   What did I do?   What did the other person do?

   What did I say?   What did the other person say?

   What did I feel?   What did I believe the other person felt and
                           what led me to that conclusion?

(2)   What conclusions can I draw?

   What could I have done and said differently?

(3)   What will I try to do next time?

While this is not particularly sophisticated, it is eminently practical for the 'beginner'.

Reflection Model II

There are more sophisticated models on which to base observations. Transactional Analysis is one. Others include the Thomas–Kilman conflict model, Belbin's team roles, assertive behaviour models, etc. A 'generic' competence model or 'personal effectiveness' model enables the learner/manager to look at his/her own behaviours in more detail.

   Michael was a planning manager with a local authority. Under re-organisation, he was due to be promoted to deal with issues of policy that would involve him working with both material and local policy makers. He felt secure with his 'technical' skills but was more concerned to establish himself as credible in the eye of others. He was shown the McBer generic competence model and decided he would use it as a checklist of personal behavioural indicators to look for. Over a period of only two months, his approach was of necessity relatively broad brush. He didn't agree with all of the model, but each time he spotted a behaviour as indicated his confidence increased as he knew he was 'on the right track'. His confidence also grew as each time he reflected on an event that went 'wrong' he was able to identify precisely which behaviours he had not displayed and so knew which ones to target next time.

- The learner/manager identifies a model of good practice and assesses his or her performance against it.
- The activities undertaken during an MLC include keeping a log of observations on a regular basis.
- The objective of the MLC becomes to improve reflection skills themselves in order to improve a person's managerial ability.

Some managers are natural reflectors, or have the self-confidence to assess their own performance honestly and openly. Other managers need to be helped.

Interventions and effect on approaches to learning

We have emphasised the need for the ownership of an MLC to remain with the learner/manager, and for the trainer to avoid directing the learner/manager. Inevitably though, the experienced trainer will have a feel in broad terms for what works and what doesn't. The issue for the experienced trainer is to decide whether to offer ideas on how to approach a particular learning topic. There are two extremes:

- *Learning objective* – to improve my ability to reduce conflict at team meetings. The learning activities require the learner/manager to research the literature on conflict in order to identify a practical strategy, prior to applying the strategy
- *Learning objective* – to improve my ability to reduce conflict at team meetings. The trainer tells the learner how conflict can be reduced, and the activities listed in the MLC are purely experiential in applying the ideas.

The first extreme takes the concept of self-discovery to its logical extent. The risk is that the learner/manager may become frustrated by having to wade through mountains of literature before finding a workable framework of ideas. The consequences of 'failing' in this MLC are that the learner/manager may lose confidence and motivation.

The second extreme has all the risks of lack of ownership. What the trainer suggests as a suitable approach may well be unsuitable to the learner/manager and the situation at hand.

Somewhere in between these two extremes lies a happy medium. Where the trainer feels a brief introduction to the topic will enable the learner/manager to take a bigger step forward, then the approach should be to lay out alternative perspectives so that the learner/manager can select a suitable approach (see Box 9.11).

When considering the range of contract opportunities, it is worthwhile developing models of approaches to common contract types. The negotiator should not attempt to force the contract to fit a model but, rather, use the model as a diagnostic aid. For example, the following different learning contracts could follow from the initial statement 'I want to improve my computer skills'.

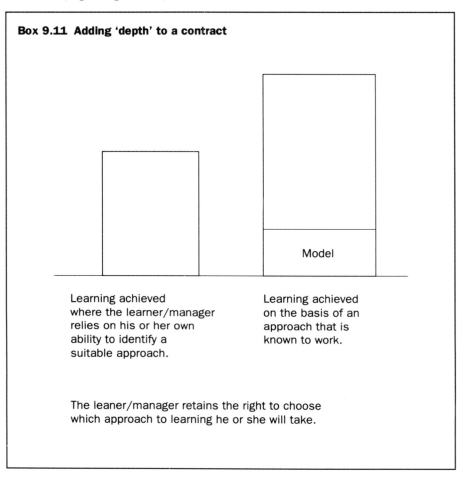

Box 9.11 Adding 'depth' to a contract

Learning achieved where the learner/manager relies on his or her own ability to identify a suitable approach.

Learning achieved on the basis of an approach that is known to work.

Model

The leaner/manager retains the right to choose which approach to learning he or she will take.

1. Develop keyboard skills – literally, finger dexterity or 'typing skills' with additional reference to special keys.

2. Computer literacy – a beginner's understanding of the component parts of computers, the software, hardware, floppy discs, etc., with an understanding of the main types of software, databases, spreadsheets and wordprocessors and possible applications.

3. The company computer – where an organisation has a customised system which the learner wishes to master.

4. (a) Using a specified piece of software – the learner may wish to get to grips with, for example, Lotus 1–2–3 in order to set up a simple spreadsheet for his/her section's budget control.

(b) Programming skills – this is a variation of 4(a) which in effect means making a standard piece of software like Lotus 1–2–3 more 'user friendly' by setting regular input or output screens.

5. Briefing a computer specialist – managers do not wish to acquire 'programming skills' (it takes a long time!), but do need to be able to identify 'inputs and outputs' required, i.e. a form of systems analysis, in order to be able to brief the professional programmer.

Computer contracts which fall outside one of the above are unlikely to meet the requirement of MLCs. All the issues concerning relevance, entry, ability and access to opportunity apply when determining the exit behaviour required. Having such models in mind help the trainer identify what the real learning objectives are.

Learning topics

Throughout this chapter, examples have been given of a wide range of MLC learning topics.

MLCs fall into three broad areas, functional, interpersonal and intrapersonal skills. Examples of some of the more common topics are given here, but it is important not to view these as a 'menu'.

Functional	Interpersonal	Intrapersonal
Informational Technology	Chairing meetings	Self-confidence
Project Management	Presentation skills	Positive attitude
Systems Analysis	Persuasion	Reflection skills
Cost/Benefit Analysis	Interviewing	Goal setting
Job Analysis	Role set analysis	Self-audit
Time Management, e.g. learning to do a task quicker	Time Management, e.g. learning to hurry up slow meetings	Time Management, e.g. reducing stress

Whereas the emphasis of any contract may fall under one of the three headings, it is inevitable, indeed preferable, that overlap should be encouraged.

While some learning topics occur regularly it is often the more unusual ones that are stimulating to the trainer.

Box 9.12 Unusual MLCs

Stan knew exactly what he wanted to learn – advanced driving skills. There may have been an element of 'testing' the management learning contract process, but he was able to justify his need by stating he spent over 40 per cent of his time on the road as an area sales engineer, and saw it as a way of reducing stress.

Sarah was particularly concerned with equal opportunity issues and wished to do an 'attitude survey' of junior and middle managers in the shops in her company's area. While developing survey skills, she was also able to influence the company in introducing a more proactive approach to equal opportunities.

John was considering taking early retirement but intended to 'keep working in some form or other if only to keep the money coming in'. He decided he needed to learn how to assess whether his 'dream' of setting up an organic vegetable business was viable.

Mike was up for promotion in a few months. He was concerned about facing the interview panel. He decided his real need was to 'learn how to be a good interviewee'.

Alan was being seconded to his company's factory in the Middle East and wanted to prepare for it. He wanted to learn some Arabic and it was agreed he would learn the basic greetings and etiquette, and a range of technical terms to provide a base for learning more conversational skills when he was there.

Summary

From this chapter, you should have a reasonable 'feel' for what is possible in an MLC and a clear idea of what limits their scope. In particular it is important to see MLCs in terms of:

- staged development
- tall and thin or short and fat
- opportunities and constraints being two sides of the same coin.

Emphasis has been given to reflection skills as being a strong force in soft skill areas, and ways have been discussed to 'add value' to learning.

Exercise

1. Why is the concept of staged development so important to an MLC?

2. What are the pitfalls a trainer may encounter when faced with a learner/manager's request to learn counselling skills?

3. How could an MLC whose main activity is a functional one of analysing a system have learning objectives targeted at interpersonal or personal skills?

Chapter 10

Case studies: systems, stress and time:

These three brief studies provide examples of the different proposals managers bring to MLCs.

Case study 1

Commencement date: 22.1.90   **Planned completion date:** 19.3.90

Goal
What is the contract about? What might be its title?

Systems Management.

Objectives
What knowledge and/or skills do you intend to gain?

To understand how the XYZ change/modification control system works.

Activities
How are you going to achieve your objectives? What tasks, projects, exercises will you do?

To seek advice and experience about current procedures, collate existing documentation on systems related to different sites.

Produce flow chart of the system and the involvement required from my site.

Resources
Resources to be used – books, audiotapes, films, people to be contacted, help you might need.

Other sites, colleagues, company documentation, myself.

Assessment
What evidence will you show to demonstrate your learning? What criteria will be used to ensure that this evidence is satisfactory?

Flow chart showing my site's involvement within the overall change control procedure.

Draft recommendation for proposed changes, identifying barriers, with justification including likely costs.

Log on how I approached the Contract, how I got the information and evaluated it. What have I learnt about myself, my skills.

Oral discussion of the log to elicit key learning points.

Background

Andrew was a 24-year-old graduate with a technical background. Often, young managers have limited perspectives of their job and potential. He worked for a Project Manager responsible for co-ordinating technical services to a range of Unit Production Managers. Whenever a product was updated, the new specification had to be recorded centrally to meet future maintenance programmes. There was a system to do this but it was not being adhered to. Andrew had been briefed by his boss to find out how the system worked, to write it up, suggest improvements and recommend a way to 'sell' it to the Unit Production Managers.

Contract negotiation

On the face of it, this appeared to be a 'project'; the trainer felt it might just be acceptable as a functional learning contract, that is 'to learn how the system worked'. On asking what activities needed to be done, it soon became clear that many more opportunities for learning existed. Since Andrew would have to 'go out' to gather information he would be improving his networking and information evaluation skills.

The wording of the learning objectives remained as set out by Andrew, even though the objectives were very limited. The trainer asked for an additional piece of assessment, a detailed log of events from which it was expected new learning would be demonstrated.

Contract assessment

Andrew had done an excellent piece of work. In this case the boss had to be the judge of the accuracy of the 'outputs', the flow chart and implementation recommendation. He was well pleased as the work 'met his requirements' and enabled him to 'go to his bosses with a clear proposal in mind'. A clear understanding of the system had been demonstrated.

Andrew then produced his log detailing the actions he had undertaken. It transpired he had considered carefully who to approach and initially targeted a supervisor 'who had been around the site for years and knew the business inside and out'. Unfortunately, the supervisor was also 'cynical about young upstarts' and 'sceptical about anything ever being done right'. Andrew spent several hours over a ten-day period 'cultivating' the supervisor, gaining his trust and commitment. In this time Andrew had to 'listen and accept' a lot of moaning about how hard done by the supervisor felt, and build up a piecemeal picture of how a changed control system would or would not work effectively.

Using this as a starting point, Andrew visited other sites, and led formal meetings with Unit Production Managers where his background knowledge, understanding of the problems faced by them, and his ability to talk their language enabled him to get their commitment to taking the change control system seriously.

The bare bones of these activities were recorded in the log but the real 'learning' was elicited in an oral discussion by the amount of skills he had unconsciously displayed. He was able to use his conclusions as a basis for discussing future tactics. He had become 'switched on to the idea that his job was not just about tasks but also about people'. In the subsequent MLC, the explicit emphasis of learning was to improve his influencing skills.

Case study 2

Commencement date: 18.8.89   **Planned completion date:** 20.9.90

Goal
What is the contract all about? What might be its title?

Stress Management.

Objectives
What knowledge and/or skills do you intend to gain?

To learn what the demands are that cause me stress.

Resources
Resources which will be used – books, audiotapes, films, people to be contacted, help you might need.

I'm OK you're OK, Thomas Harris. *Assertiveness at Work,* Kate and Ken Back. Myself.

Activities

How are you going to achieve your objectives? What tasks, projects, exercises will you do?

Take 15 minutes at lunch and before I go home to reflect on key events in the previous few hours. (Use the reflection model; ensure no distraction.)

Write up reflections and specify conclusions. Read two books.

Assessment

What evidence will you show to demonstrate your learning? What criteria will be used to ensure that this evidence is satisfactory?

Log of reflection using Reflection Model. List of conclusions. Action plan of what I need to develop in myself and suggestions as to how I can reach them.

Oral discussion with trainer and line manager of what I have learnt about myself and what I am doing differently.

Background

Susan worked in the Personnel Department of a local authority. She was middle-aged, recently divorced and came across to the trainer as 'highly-strung'. Her boss appeared to be one of those people with 'an iron hand in a velvet glove'.

Contract negotiation

The opening encounter between Susan, her boss and the trainer to negotiate the first MLC was not comfortable. There was clearly a great deal of tension between Susan and her boss which was blocking any progress with the MLC. The contract negotiation was in danger of leading to open conflict.

The trainer, being very careful not to direct the conversation, eventually managed to get Susan to say she was 'feeling very stressed with all the demands put on her'. The underlying message was that she saw her boss as the main stress factor. The boss said and did nothing to suggest he had heard this or indeed any other messages.

There were two opportunities arising from this encounter: first Susan could learn to reduce the stress she was feeling and, second, she could begin to learn how to look at transactions in behavioural terms thereby improving her ability to discuss events more rationally with her boss. The trainer felt it would be inappropriate to outline these opportunities as they could be misinterpreted, and therefore opted for another approach.

The trainer said at this point that he wasn't getting a clear picture of what Susan wanted and would feel happier if she could identify what the demands were that caused her stress. This could become the 'learning objective'. He then described how he himself often found it useful to spend 15 minutes at lunch-time and before going home looking back at what happened previously. He described the reflection model he used (see Reflection Model I p. 190) to come to 'real' conclusions, Susan picked up on this immediately; the boss was also keen as, it is believed, he saw it as a way of making Susan less highly strung.

In addition to a log of reflections, the trainer suggested two books *Assertiveness at Work* by Kate and Ken Back and *I'm OK You're OK* by Thomas Harris, as 'good but easy to read books that may give some ideas as to what to look for'.

Contract assessment

At the assessment session, the first thing the trainer noticed was a significant change in interactions between Susan and her boss. They were not necessarily 'warm and friendly' but sharp and businesslike. Whereas before Susan had a tendency to 'avoid' her boss, keeping her eyes and body turned away and voice low, she was now prepared to face him and make sure she was heard. The boss was responding positively to this assertive behaviour and had stopped 'cloaking' his iron hand. The trainer was pleased to see 'real' communication beginning with both parties establishing their rights.

Susan produced her log. She had stuck to the timetable and procedure. Apart from several operational conclusions on work practices, her main conclusion was that by clearly identifying what had happened and her role in each event she had 'stopped dwelling on things that went wrong'. People with high activist-reflector preferences and low theorist preferences like Susan can self-destruct unless they get a grip on real behaviours.

In addition, the simple activity of 'stopping the world' regularly meant she was more relaxed during the day. The two books, although not central to the MLC, had provided her with an insight that managing herself and other people was a possibility, and it was clear that she was already applying some of the ideas.

The trainer didn't want to push any of these points too far, not with the boss present. The MLC had in effect been a key for setting up subsequent contracts.

Case study 3

Commencement date: 8.1.90   **Planned completion date:** 15.3.90

Goal
What is the contract all about? What might be its title?

Time Management.

Objectives
What knowledge and/or skills do you intend to gain?

To learn how to plan my time. To be able to inform other people of my workload.

Resources
Resources which will be used – books, audiotapes, films, people to be contacted, help you might need.

Time planning sheets.

Activities
How are you going to achieve your objectives? What tasks, projects, experiences, exercises will you do?

Complete time planning sheets for one month – list tasks for month, weeks and days, prioritise using ABCX, estimate times.

Reflect on accuracy of estimations and reasons why tasks done/not done.

Assessment
What evidence will you show to demonstrate your learning? What criteria will be used to ensure that this evidence is satisfactory?

Time planning sheets and comments.

Oral discussion of how I've improved and identify which jobs I can now accurately estimate times for, which are important, which are urgent.

Oral account of how I presented my workload to others.

Background

Ron worked in the accounts department for a large ex-public utility. He had been average in the work he had done previously on the

Certificate in Management Studies programme he was taking. He seemed settled, or even resigned, in his job and did not show any proactivity.

Contract negotiation

Ron arrived at the meeting without his boss. The two of them had talked about MLC ideas and the boss had 'told' him to improve his time management. Ron passively accepted this.

The trainer asked Ron to describe his job, the key requirements and deadlines. It came out that Ron met the requirements and didn't miss deadlines. More pertinently, Ron said his boss often dropped work on his desk at short notice causing Ron to become flustered and to give the appearance of not managing his time. This is a common event where a person needs to be able to say to his or her boss 'this is what I have on my schedule; if you give me that extra work what would you like me to postpone?'

The MLC therefore had two purposes: to plan activities by prioritising them in terms of urgency versus importance and learning to estimate how long a task would take in real time, and then to use this as 'evidence' when negotiating work with the boss.

Contract assessment

Ron had 'religiously' used the simple but effective model of time planning offered by the trainer. He was able to justify why he categorised any task as urgent and/or important, and was now 'in control' of his job. As a by-product, he had even built in time for other activities such as reading his professional journals, getting more hands-on experience of computers, etc.

In addition to this increase in control and proactivity, Ron was exhilarated now that his boss came and asked what he had scheduled before handing over work.

Review

One of these contracts was virtually a project proposal at its inception, and on the surface it remained a contract about acquiring knowledge, but its effects were far more wide-reaching.

One contract was undertaken by a manager unwillingly at the insistence of his boss. In this case some positive results were produced, but this is not always so.

One contract was an attempt to address what appeared to be the principal problem affecting a manager, and is a clear example of the 'staged progress' approach of effective MLCs.

Chapter 11

Case studies: impact, interviews and motivation

Three more case studies illustrate the ways managers may choose to explore and develop interpersonal skills through Management Learning Contracts.

Case study 4

Commencement date: 18.10.89   **Planned completion date:** 15.12.89

Goal
What is the contract about? What might be its title?

Making an impact.

Objectives
What knowledge and/or skills do you intend to gain?

To identify a range of techniques to help me in my role as a planning manager.

To identify and improve personal skills and 'scripts' to introduce these techniques into planning meetings.

Resources
Resources which will be used – books, audiotapes, films, people to be contacted, help you might need.

Management Teams Belbin. *What is Management?* and *Operations Management* NRMC. Personal Effectiveness Model MCI

Activities
How are you going to achieve your objectives? What tasks, projects, experiences, exercises will you do?

Complete 'Operations Management'. Revise the 'Management Teams' and identify possible scripts to intervene in appropriate role.

Use above and Personal Effectiveness model to prepare and reflect on own effectiveness at meetings.

Assessment

What evidence will you show to demonstrate your learning? What criteria will be used to ensure that this evidence is satisfactory?

Checklist of techniques and their uses.

Preparation and reflection notes on meetings attended.

Identifying my purpose and scripts to use – on a rolling basis.

Written self-assessment of my performance showing where I have gained and where I need to develop.

Checklist of skills and qualities required in an effective planning manager.

Background

George was one of several analysts in a local authority Social Services Department responsible for assessing the implications of central government directives and making recommendations. The local authority was going through a period of considerable re-organisation and George's job was due to be 'rationalised'. George did not have a boss at that moment but was currently reporting directly to the Chief Officer.

Contract negotiation

George had shown himself in a previous MLC to be a very thoughtful person, able to assess accurately his own abilities. He was not unduly worried about the re-organisation as he knew he would be in a job 'of some sort'. On starting the discussion he began by saying he saw the re-organisation as an opportunity to gain more responsibility and maybe to 'create a job' more suitable to his talents. He felt though that he needed to be able to 'come across better to the politicians' who would ultimately be responsible for his fate.

He described how he was a member of regular planning meetings that local councillors attended, and that he wished to use the opportunity to make more of an impact.

With diagnostic questioning, three issues came to light; the sort of roles he could take at the meetings, the planning skills he could bring to the meetings, for example problem analysis skills, and the skills or approaches needed to do these effectively.

On the face of it, this was potentiallly a huge MLC, but George had already shown considerable learning ability and could take on new ideas quickly. However, the trainer was careful not to overload George with unnecessary readings, but suggested instead an introductory reading of Belbin's team role theories, a revision of problem-solving and decision-making techniques and a reading of the model of personal effectiveness.

Contract assessment

George produced all the evidence required at assessment. He produced his preparation notes for the meetings and reflection notes assessing his 'performance'. What he discovered was that his planning skills were and had been for some time perfectly sound but that by crystallising a range of techniques in his mind he was more confident about introducing them to the meetings.

He had found Belbin's theories useful in deciding what sort of intervention was appropriate, and he had found the model of Personal Effectiveness useful as a guiding framework to develop 'scripts' to make the intervention work.

This was a sort of 'rolling contract' where improvement is continuous. The limit of improvement was only determined by the cut-off date of assessment. As a result of the MLC, George noted that he was being 'turned to more and more' as the person who was able to 'get things going'. Councillors were also seeking his advice more outside the meetings.

By establishing his credibility and by being able to articulate what he saw as the requirements of a good planner, George was promoted a few months later.

Case study 5

Commencement date: 15.3.90   **Planned completion date:** 15.4.90

Goal
What is the contract all about? What might be its title?

To develop selection interview skills and use in a 'live' situation.

Objectives
What knowledge and/or skills do you intend to gain?

Learn to use the 7 point plan.

How to prepare employee specifications.

Develop, question and listening techniques to get the best out of the candidate.

Learn to use and recognise non-verbal signs.

Resources
Resources which will be used – books, audiotapes, films, people to be contacted, help you might need.

Active listening readings.

Personnel.

Aids from training college – videos/books.

'More than a gut feeling', Melrose video.

Activities
How are you going to achieve your objectives? What tasks, projects, experiences, exercises will you do?

Obtain copies of the 7 point plan and talk to Personnel about them.

Interrogate sample employee specifications.

Watch selection interview videos.

Run the interviews for trainee computer operators – two vacancies.

Assessment
What evidence will you show to demonstrate your learning? What criteria will be used to ensure that this evidence is satisfactory?

Preparation materials:
  – employee specification
  – strategies for questions to extract information.

Log of each interview:

(a) panel reflections on interviews
(b) additional reflections of my own performance – what could I have done/said differently?

Written report on how and why I justified my selection to the rest of the panel.

Observations from panel on my performance and what I have learnt about myself.

Background

Alison was a recently appointed manager in a growing computer department. She had been asked to organise quickly the recruitment and selection of two trainees. Like many in this situation she had no training; she was, however, sufficiently concerned to want to learn and to prepare as best she could, so chose an MLC in selection interviewing on a 'crash course' basis.

Contract negotiation

The constraints of time meant the MLC had to be essentially about Action. Additionally, developing interpersonal skills means that, whatever simulations or practice sessions one might have, real evidence only comes from real situations. The trainer therefore advised Alison that the interviews had to be as 'safe' as possible.

He outlined three 'environmental' factors conducive to developing interpersonal skills in a real situation; the risks of getting it wrong must be minimised, the risks of emotions getting in the way of rational thinking have to be minimised, and a slower pace or rather extra time must be allowed for writing the situation itself. Additionally, having a sound framework or plan to hold onto when events are not working out is useful.

It was therefore agreed at the negotiation to take these issues into consideration when determining what actions should be taken. The framework or plan was provided by the NRMC book, *Managing People*. This does not attempt to turn novices into skilled interviewers overnight but gives a clear simple structure of job description leading to employee specification leading to interviewing strategy. In order to make this structure workable, Alison said she would get detailed advice from Personnel.

To support this, she planned to watch the video 'More than a gut feeling' by Melrose and go through the accompanying handbook to develop a line of questioning to target interviewees' past behaviour. This was the only preparation she would have time for.

As far as the three environmental factors were concerned, Alison said she would get someone from Personnel and a more experienced colleague to sit in with her during the interviews. Their role would be firstly to ensure no bad mistakes were made and secondly to act as observers of her performance. She agreed to provide them with a specific checklist of things to look for. Finally, she agreed to give herself a minimum of 15 minutes between interviews to collect her thoughts, reflect on what worked and what didn't and to receive some quick feedback from her observers. While this may not be ideal, the trainer felt it was the best possible line of action given the constraints. It was agreed she would write up a detailed review at a more leisurely time later and produce a detailed action plan of knowledge and skills she would have to learn before next time.

Contract assessment

Alison was very pleased at the way the interviews had gone. She said she had felt more confident at least knowing what she should be trying to do. The employee specification had worked well enough but she intended next time to think through in more detail areas such as 'be able to use one's initiative' and 'be able to fit in with a team'. She was able to produce detailed observations of specific events and drew reasonable conclusions about which questions and approach worked best for her. The success of the MLC was not so much based on whether Alison had progressed her skills and knowledge, as on an audit and awareness of her current level.

Case study 6

Commencement date: 7.2.90   **Planned completion date:** 31.3.90

Goal
What is the contract all about? What might be its title?

Motivation.

Objectives
What knowledge and/or skills do you intend to gain?

To learn why lateness/absenteeism levels are 'high'.

To find ways to reduce levels of absenteeism/sickness.

Resources
Resources which will be used – books, audiotapes, films, people to be contacted, help you might need.

Activities
How are you going to achieve your objectives? What tasks, projects, experiences, exercises will you do?

Compare records of my unit with others.

Research articles, short readings on causes of absenteeism/sickness.

List what I am looking for and speak to Personnel and ACAS people how best to get it. Interview my targeted staff to identify their reasons without causing upset.

Assessment

What evidence will you show to demonstrate your learning? What criteria will be used that this evidence is satisfactory?

Written summary report from readings on the main theories identifying causes of lateness/absenteeism.

Records comparing my unit with others, with brief analysis.

Findings from interviews (based on a structured approach from readings).

Proposals for reducing absenteeism/lateness – justify for realism.

Oral account of how I interviewed people, how I handled resistance, how I was constructive.

Background

Graham managed a production line making components that were assembled with other production line components into the finished goods. He had a good deal of autonomy over work schedules, manning levels, etc., and his only brief in effect was to produce a certain number a day. His main concern at the time of the MLC was the time he was having to spend sorting out problems caused by absenteeism and lateness. He wanted to 'knock a few heads together'.

Graham appeared to the trainer to be a very confident manager. He was task driven, technically sound, and 'knew' what he wanted. He didn't show, however, any sign of having considered any of the possible causes of absenteeism and lateness, thinking only that the work-force were 'a shiftless bunch'. In this respect he fitted the stereotype of a 'Theory X' manager.

Contract negotiation

The learning objectives were quite straightforward. The trainer felt though that the process might be more problematical; the problem was whether Graham could now talk to people about their absenteeism without it developing into a judgemental and recriminating session. The risk of that happening with Graham seemed high.

Without labouring the point, the trainer asked Graham to consider the consequences of taking a wrong approach to tackling the problem. Graham soon realised that he ought to get advice first, and with little prompting he said he would 'talk it over with the Personnel Department'. With Graham now beginning to show willingness to think before acting, the trainer offered two other sources of information, articles from various personnel magazines and the local ACAS office. The trainer believed that any more information inputs would 'overload' Graham until he had had the chance to test out a few ideas for himself. He felt that, at the very least, Graham couldn't do any greater damage than if he hadn't done any thinking at all beforehand. At the very best, Graham would begin to evaluate thoroughly his one-sided approach to managing people.

Contract assessment

One of the benefits of task driven people is that they can usually be relied on to go out and 'do'! Graham had certainly done that, treating the MLC like some sort of battle campaign. He had found the advice and ideas from the journals and ACAS 'solid, no-nonsense stuff'.

His approach to the interviews was 'as normal to get straight to the point with no pussy-footing'. However, following the advice he had been given, he did not 'jump to conclusions' and did not 'condemn them', but said to the interviewees he wanted them 'to do the talking and to say what they thought about the situation'. In other words, without really understanding the theory, or even wanting to understand the theory, he had changed his normal approach to a more effective one, strictly for pragmatic reasons.

While his proposals for reducing absenteeism might not have been to everyone's taste, he was already putting them into practice and finding them successful. The trainer did not expect to change a person's basic nature to one more in line with his own thinking, but was pleased to note that Graham included several statements in the assessment discussion showing he was listening to his operators more carefully.

Review

Each of these contracts involved some exploration and assessment of interpersonal skills. The examples illustrate how the specific needs and the immediate environment of the manager may have a considerable effect on the direction and detail of the contract, so that the resulting agreement and activity are designed for each individual.

Part Four

The future

Chapter 12

The learning organisation

When you have completed this chapter you should be able to:

- **explain how Management Learning Contracts can help develop the organisation.**
- **give examples of how MLCs could be used within your own organisation.**

Introduction

For years people have been talking about the Learning Organisation, but no one is sure of what it is or how it can be developed. The idea first arose in the context of organisations needing to be adaptive to cope with change (*Schon 1972*) and for the individuals who make up the organisation to approach change in a positive manner, and to learn the new facts and skills necessary to meet the challenge of changed demands. This is an attractive idea, waiting only for the means to implement it.

The Management Learning Contract method can play a substantial role in developing the Learning Organisation. It is not the only tool which is necessary, however: it may not even be the main tool for any particular organisation: it would be dangerous to regard it as a cure-all method.

In the preceding chapters we have discussed ideas and approaches which have been tried and tested. In this chapter let us explore some speculations about what may happen in the future.

The learning organisation

There are certain features of the Learning Organisation on which there is general agreement:

It is dealing with change. The change area may be felt in the market, or in other changing demands on the organisation, or in the supply of resources – people or materials – on which the organisation depends; the origins of change may be political, economic, social or technological.

It looks outward, and forward. In particular, the values of the organisation promote a concern with customer needs *(Peters and Waterman 1982)* and an involvement of all employees in the aim of satisfying the customer. This is not frozen at a point in time; it entails asking what will happen next month, next quarter, next year, and so on.

It encourages a positive attitude towards individual learning. This is done by a variety of means to create an atmosphere conducive to individual development.

It uses coaching by line managers to develop staff. This is a route towards relating learning directly to the real needs of the job and of the organisation. The Learning Organisation therefore encourages and rewards line managers who develop and train their subordinates.

Box 12.1 Positive attitudes

Aspects of encouraging a positive attitude to individual learning would include:
- explicit recognition that everyone has something to learn
- identification of personal learning needs and progress towards meeting them is encouraged
- there is a recognition of learning opportunities
- senior managers accept and make positive statements about their own learning needs: upward communication is encouraged
- curiosity and innovation are encouraged
- failure (in operational terms) is tolerated

The other dimensions of the Learning Organisation are either less clearly defined, or they are the subject of debate, with perhaps one important exception. Whatever features are embodied in the Learning Organisation, they are part of the value system of that organisation. We are no longer lodged within the confines of what in many organisations is the present-day situation, of trainers seeking to make management development programmes more effective. We are operating within a corporate culture that values both change and learning, and provides support to individual efforts to manage change and to engage in self-development, and the development of others, by a range of means, from the commendation of senior managers on public occasions to the availability of basic resources needed for learning.

Box 12.2 Lip service

Company A makes a public display of concern for management development. The Personnel Director speaks at local conferences on the latest thinking about learning to manage innovation. Money is made available for junior managers to undertake competence development programmes, but they experience frequent difficulties in attending because of operational pressures. Immediate activities and short-term needs are always given precedence by middle managers over longer-term development needs.

Company B is also prominent in management development. It provides resources (including a relaxation of operational pressures) and support. But senior managers not directly involved in the management development process have a habit of revealing, through public addresses or through speeches to learners/managers, their personal ignorance of key aspects of the development process.

Both of these companies are more advanced than Company C, which makes no pretence to develop managers and allocates no resources to this purpose, but Companies A and B still have some way to go before they can regard themselves as Learning Organisations.

MLCs and the learning organisation

Certain features of the MLC approach are of practical value in developing the Learning Organisation.

- Any area of learning and development can be addressed by a Management Learning Contract. So an MLC can provide the link between any organisational needs and individual development. MLCs have been used at all levels within organisations, from senior managers to potential supervisors.
- Within this great flexibility, a Management Learning Contract has a firm structure, with clear definitions of objectives and performance measures, which can support learning and guide assessment.
- The MLC approach harnesses the energy and the expertise of the individual learner, so that the aims and activities of a contract should be relevant to the learning needs of the individual in his/her job. If this is the case, learning becomes a dimension of the job as relevant as any other aspect of performance – not a luxury, or an excursion, or a matter of personal interest. Success and failure might reasonably be followed by the same kind of consequences that attend success or failure in any other aspect of performance.
- Management Learning Contracts can involve the learner's line manager in the development process, in a well-defined role. An

MLC approach, correctly applied, can ensure that line managers have a clear brief on what they are expected to do (see above, Chapter 8). This clarity, structure and support can overcome some of the natural resistance to involvement in coaching.

- The expertise of specialists can be applied to a manager's development through the MLC method – whether in the form of the personal development expertise of a company trainer, or an expert in finance, computing, legislation, foreign languages, and so on, who can be involved in the contract by the trainer and learner.

These features are valuable in developing individuals to meet organisational needs.

Limitations

Of course, the Management Learning Contract approach is not sufficient to bring about the Learning Organisation, nor is it the sole recommended approach to management development in the future. We must be careful not to rely too heavily on one method, or to try to force everything we want from training and development into this one mould.

In an organisation faced with changing circumstances – one of the dimensions of the Learning Organisation – procedures for scanning the change areas, and for communicating results of these surveys, need to be established, and methods of allocating responsibilities to establish an organic, flexible organisation are appropriate. These measures go beyond the individual focus of the Management Learning Contract Approach.

Turning to individual learning, at least two other methods, besides the MLC of shaping development must be given distinct recognition.

First, in some cases an entire group of managers will have common learning needs. Perhaps a new level in the hierarchy is now required to carry out appraisal interviews, or perhaps Team Briefing has been introduced as a system of cascade communication, or maybe some fundamental change in information technology results in common training needs for a group of staff. In these circumstances the training department may be charged with devising an introductory package to the new skills, activities for the learners to carry out, perhaps even ways in which learners' skills can be assessed during or after the programme. It may be entirely appropriate to set standard activities and standard assignments (see Box 12.3).

Management Learning Contracts are appropriate when the learning

---

Box 12.3 The quality assignment

An Action Assignment used in connection with a short Total Quality Management training course asked participants to undertake the following tasks:
- Write down examples of waste/re-work in your department.
- Select two of these and suggest how improvements could be made.

This should direct learners to consider activities that are relevant to them and their job, and a structure for the inquiry is provided, but this is essentially an assignment (or a small project) and not a Management Learning Contract, and the two should not be confused.

---

needs of individual managers are different from one another. When new skills or techniques are introduced, the difference between learning needs may be negligible, and a standard activity may be more suitable. It is important to gauge the circumstances correctly.

Secondly, an aspect of the Learning Organisation is that its members look to make changes and improvements in organisational methods and systems. In particular, at present there is a strong emphasis on quality, on meeting customer requirements, producing goods and services to the correct specification, identifying barriers to customer satisfaction, reducing unnecessary costs.

This results in a focus on systems and procedures, and on making recommendations for change. This can be valuable in making the organisation more effective, but it is not Management Learning Contract activity, as we have defined it here. It bears a closer relationship to Project work (see Chapter 5, above). The two approaches can exist side by side, and one can benefit the other. Their precise relationship in any particular scheme must be explored, however, and carefully explained because they should on no account be mistaken for one another.

Specific applications

Some preparation of the learner/manager is necessary if the Management Learning Contract is to be used effectively (as we saw in Chapter 4) and this means setting the MLC in a particular context, at least for its initial use. In the previous chapters of this book we have drawn on examples of MLCs used as part of management development and training programmes.

Undoubtedly the simplest way of introducing MLCs into an organisation is as an element in the training department's short course provision, connecting two or more group meetings or workshops and enabling practical competence development on the job in the interim. (See Box 7.5 for an example of a programme structured in this way.)

This introduces learners/managers to MLCs, makes space for application of any workshop principles to real practice, and shifts the focus of short course training to action and to assessment of outputs – that is, skilled behaviours – rather than discussion and a counting of inputs. It retains the central advantage of the MLC approach, of course, in that it enables each learner/manager to take an individual approach to skill development and so design a personal programme suited to his/her needs and opportunities.

Box 12.4 Common roots

It may be appropriate to follow a short course based on organisational needs with individual MLCs although it is more likely that a directive assignment of some sort will be more effective in establishing a foundation of the skills needed by the organisation than a contract.

Suppose an organisation introduces Team Briefing and provides short training courses, followed by some work-place activity, for Briefers.

An assignment approach directs the learners to carry out certain activities (which may include carrying out a briefing and also reflecting on it).

An MLC approach asks the learner what he/she will do to improve his/her Team Briefing skills, and requires a clear, justifiable proposal of the particular skills the individual will develop – how he/she will do this, and how that achievement should be measured.

In cases of this kind careful design of the parameters of the MLC is necessary to ensure that individual and organisational needs are met.

This method of first use of MLCs has the additional advantage of providing a supportive setting for the development of the trainer skills that are an essential component of effective contracting.

Additional specific applications concern:

- Individual weaknesses
- Job rotation/placements
- Succession planning
- Managing change.

Let us take a brief look at each of these in turn.

Individual weaknesses can be addressed by Management Learning Contracts in any context, of course, including the short course and training context mentioned above. Where individual weaknesses are identified by the organisation's system of appraisal, or of staff development, or simply by a line manager conscientiously assessing the strengths and needs of his/her staff, an MLC can be an ideal means of helping the individual to develop. As we saw in Chapter 3, there is a tendency for appraisal systems on the MbO model to concentrate on results in the form of quantifiable production and/or on learning as inputs (numbers of courses attended), and neither of these approaches has a focus so well defined or so supportive as a Management Learning Contract.

If the MLC approach is to be used in this way it will probably need to be:

- as a service offered by the training department to line managers in connection with the appraisal and development of their staff.
- carefully explained to line managers, in terms both of its power and of its limitations (as in Chapter 8, above).
- offered to line managers as a method they can use themselves (without the intervention of the training department) in the future, if they wish.

Job rotation/placements form part of the management development programmes of some companies, particularly for managers who are expected to fulfil promising potential. Management Learning Contracts may be used here to clarify what the individual is expected to gain from the job change, and to make explicit afterwards what he/she has in fact gained, and to turn the focus more on outputs – in the sense of skills developed, knowledge acquired, competences attained – rather than on the inputs of time spent gaining experience of a particular job. Management Learning Contracts can increase the likelihood of a placement being of benefit – and can, in any case, assess how much benefit has been derived.

Difficulties with the use of MLCs in this context revolve around the extent to which the demands and opportunities presented by the placement are unknown or unpredictable, and the timescale of the experience. Trainers who use job rotations or placements as a regular means of management development should remember that ownership of the MLC by the learner/manager is a key feature of the approach discussed in this book. The manager must know enough about the demands and opportunities of his/her environment to make realistic proposals. After this initial familiarisation has taken place, a contract could be agreed. Where placements (or rotations) last for six months or longer perhaps two or more sequential contracts should be established.

Succession planning should entail a comparison of an individual's profile of competences with a map of the competences considered necessary to carry out a particular job, leading to an individual development plan. The value of the MLC method in this context should be obvious: the use of contracts should ensure a focus on precise and relevant skills and knowledge and on realistic methods of assessing development. The development plan, and the ensuing programme, could be spread over a relatively long term, encompassing a number of MLCs and other activities.

Finally, it is possible to envisage groups of managers using the MLC approach to manage change.

Change necessarily means a manager needs to:

- find and interpret new information and/or
- identify and analyse new problems and/or
- take new courses of action and/or
- meet and manage new people and/or
- ask people to do new things and/or
- behave in new ways in familiar situations and/or
- behave in familiar ways in new situations.

In each case there is a component of learning, which may be foreseeable, and which the manager may be able to define in advance. If the change is over a longer period of time and (relatively) controlled, the manager's efforts may be supported by the training courses and individual counselling we have already mentioned. Where the changes are shorter term, support may be more limited and the scope for planning and slow deliberation of contract proposals before agreement with a trainer may become a forgone luxury.

It is possible to envisage managers who have used MLCs on training and development programmes, turning to the method here, seeking some assistance from equally experienced colleagues, offering it in turn. Where the desired skill, the necessary knowledge, the required competence to manage a new set of circumstances can be identified, and means of achieving it planned out, managers have a sound starting point for seeking help, giving help and helping themselves in matters of development.

This final stage will not be reached without using MLCs in a more formal setting, in training and development, because only in that setting is the approach applied with sufficient discipline to produce effective Management Learning Contracts. The best process of introducing MLCs into an organisation, to help create a Learning Organisation, is likely to follow a path similar to the description just given: first used in group training programmes as a component of short courses, then used to counsel and develop individuals outside the context of a training course, and then used for the longer-term purposes of structuring job rotation or placements, and of succession planning. At each stage more members of the organisation come into contact with the method. If it is being used correctly, they place their confidence in it and learn how to use it, and encourage their colleagues to do the same.

Summary

In this chapter we have speculated on the role the Management Learning Contract might play in developing the Learning Organisation. In the Learning Organisation a high value is placed on individual learning as a means of managing change. Specifically:

- the organisation encourages a positive attitude towards individual learning
- learning is seen as part of the job, so line management is involved in guiding its direction.

We had seen from previous chapters that the flexibility of the MLC approach, together with its firm structure and the scope for involving the learner and his/her manager in designing and assessing learning, make MLCs a valuable component of the Learning Organisations.

The MLC approach alone is insufficient to bring about or implement the Learning Organisation:

- the values of the Learning Organisation need to be supported from the top of the hierarchy.
- systems and procedures to scan change areas and to exchange information are necessary if the organisation is genuinely operating in changeable circumstances.

In addition, two other methods of structuring individual learning may be of use, and they should be clearly distinguished from the MLC:

- the assignment
- the quality improvement project.

Finally, we considered the context within which MLCs might operate:

- within training programmes
- as a means of individual development, perhaps linked to appraisal
- to structure placements or maximise learning from job rotation
- as a means of succession planning
- ultimately, as a means by which managers habitually plan and evaluate their needs in changing circumstances.

Answers and references

Chapter 1 Competences: qualities and skills

Answers

1. The behaviours linked with Proactivity and Self-Confidence in the AMA research were:

Proactivity
a. Initiates new actions, communications, proposals, meetings or directives to accomplish a task; and/or
b. Initiates the new action in a task sequence, rather than waiting to react to the situation as it develops; and/or
c. Seeks information, on his or her own initiative, from a wide variety of sources concerning an issue or problem. Sources may be those identified specifically for this task or previously known but ingenuity is shown in applying them to this task; and/or
d. Identifies and takes two or more actions on his or her own initiative to solve a problem or overcome an obstacle to task performance; and/or
e. Takes calculated risks and admits and accepts personal responsibility for success or failure of those actions intended to solve a problem or achieve a goal.

Self-Confidence
a. Consistently presents himself or herself, verbally and non-verbally, in an assured, forceful, impressive and unhesitating manner; and/or
b. Consistently expresses little ambivalence about decisions that he or she has made; and/or
c. Consistently expresses the belief that he or she will succeed at a task.

2. The advantages of using a generic model in your own organisation as a basis for management development will probably revolve around the time and effort that has already been put into the research and development of the model.

The main disadvantage is likely to be the resistance of members of the organisation to a formal model (which was Not Invented Here). Of course it is also possible that the work of your organisation is so unusual that a generic model would require considerable alteration before it was suitable.

References

AMA 1982. *The Generic Competency Model*, American Management Association, 1982.

Barnard 1948. *Organisation and Management*, Chester Barnard, 1948, Harvard University Press.

Boyatzis 1982. *The Competent Manager*, Richard E. Boyatzis, 1982, Wiley.

Cockerill 1989. 'The kind of competences needed for rapid change', Tony Cockerill. *Personnel Management*, September 1989.

Deloitte, Haskins and Sells 1989. *Management Challenge for the 1990s*, Deloitte, Haskins and Sells, 1989, Training Agency.

Flanagan 1954. 'The critical incident technique', J.C. Flanagan. *Psychological Bulletin*, 1954, 51(4)

Glaze 1989. 'Cadbury's dictionary of competence', Tony Glaze. *Personnel Management*, July 1989.

Goodge and Griffiths 1985. 'Assessment Techniques: A Review', P. Goodge and P. Griffiths. *Management Education and Development*, Vol. 16 Part 3.

Greatrex and Phillips 1989. 'Oiling the wheels of competence', Julian Greatrex and Peter Phillips. *Personnel Management*, 1989.

Green 1987. 'Matching people to jobs: an expert system approach', Hugh Green. *Personnel Management*, September 1987.

Griffiths and Allen 1987. 'Assessment centres: Breaking with Tradition', P. Griffiths and B. Allen. *Journal of Management Development*, 1985, 16(3).

Helps 1872. *Thoughts upon Government*, Sir Arthur Helps. Reprinted in *Style in Administration*, R.A. Chapman and Andrew Dunsire, 1971, Allen & Unwin.

Hirsh and Bevan 1988. *What Makes a Manager?* Wendy Hirsh and Stephen Bevan, 1988, Institute of Manpower Studies.

Klemp 1980. *The Assessment of Occupational Competence*, G.O. Klemp, Jnr, 1980. Cited in Boyatzis, 1982.

Klemp 1986. 'Executive Competence: What characterises intelligent functioning among senior managers?', G.O. Klemp, Jnr and David C. McClelland, in R.J. Sternberg and R.K. Wagner, *Practical Intelligence: Nature and origins of competence in the everyday world*, 1986, Cambridge University Press.

Kolb 1976. *Learning Style Inventory*, David Kolb, 1976, McBer & Co, Boston.

Langford 1979. 'Managerial Effectiveness: A Review of the Literature', Vicky Langford, in *Managerial Effectiveness*, eds Brodie and Bennett, 1979, Thames Valley RMC.

McClelland 1953. *The Achievement Motive*, D.C. McClelland, J.W. Atkinson, R.A. Clark and E.L. Lowell, 1953, Appleton-Century.

McClelland 1958. 'Measuring Motivation', D.C. McClelland, in *Motives in Fantasy, Action and Society*, ed. J.W. Atkinson, 1988, Van Nostrand.

McClelland 1961. *The Achieving Society*, D.C. McClelland, 1961, Van Nostrand.

McClelland 1973. 'Testing for competence rather than intelligence', D.C. McClelland, *American Psychologist*, 1973, 28(1).

McGregor 1961. *The Human Side of Enterprise*, Douglas McGregor, 1961, McGraw-Hill.

Powers 1987. 'Enhancing Managerial Competence: the American Management Association Competency Programme', Edward A. Powers, *Journal of Management Development*, 1987, 6(4).

Smith and Blackham 1988. 'The Measurement of Managerial Abilities in an Assessment Centre', David Smith and Barry Blackham, *Personnel Review*, 1988, 17(4).

Thornton and Byham 1982. *Assessment Centres and Managerial Performance*, George C. Thornton III and William C. Byham, 1982, Academic Press, London.

Chapter 2 Competence standards

Answers

1. Standards can be used in a number of ways by companies. Some of the possible uses are given below. This list is unlikely to be exhaustive and there may be other uses which you have thought of which are not covered here.

- job specifications
- to provide the objectives of training and development or work objectives
- to monitor performance against development or work objectives
- for job appraisal
- to evaluate development and training programmes against organisational objectives
- to monitor and identify personnel requirements and shortages
- criteria for selection for jobs, education or training
- as a self-reflective and assessment tool for individual managers so that they become reflective practitioners
- to raise the quality of training and development and help it fit organisational requirements
- to link internal organisational training into the public infrastructure, once NVQs are up and running
- to relate individual goals to organisational requirements
- job evaluation
- to help companies meet standards specified in contract/tendering requirements.

2. Your response to this will very much depend on the internal environment of your organisation, its immediate and long-term plans and needs, the position which you hold to influence and change the way it works and the key issues for which solutions are needed.

Two possible ideas may be:

a. The key problem facing your organisation at the moment is that managers appear to have different views of what their job entails and how their work relates to the overall purpose of the organisation. A potential method for tackling this would be through setting up a series of workshops to try to identify the standards which the organisation expects of its managers. Your key reason for the workshops is not so much the final outcome of the standards, although this will have a long-term use, but that the managers will make explicit their assumptions and reflect on each other's views. This should in its turn lead to an increase in the quality of their work.

b. You work in an organisation which is based in a fast changing environment. Many of the staff, particularly the new recruits, have been complaining to their managers that they are unsure what their job actually entails and what they are supposed to do. You have been asked to sort this out and give staff a clearer idea of their job functions, the standards expected of them, the boundaries of their action and how they link with other staff.

You decide that rather than trying to explain this through the usual means such as organisational charts, you will use standards as the unifying theme. The development of standards will initially be undertaken with the new recruits. While this may have drawbacks in terms of the fullness of information which they are able to offer, it will have the advantage of engaging the newcomers in a real process and gain their commitment to the company. Where they need to find out further information on job boundaries and relations with other staff, this can be undertaken as part of their induction training, for which you already have a budget and which will take you away from a reliance on chalk and talk methods. You intend to use the outcomes in the long term as a means of developing job appraisal which you have on your own job target agenda.

References

BSD/ITS 1990. 'Quality in Training: a UK response', Barbara Shelborn Developments and Industrial Training Services, 1990. Commentary to the CEDEFOP for the Quality in Training Conference, Budapest.

Dept. of Employment 1981. *A New Training Initiative: An agenda for Action*, December, 1981, HMSO Cmnd. 8455.

Mansfield 1987. *Defining the New Standards*, Bob Mansfield, 1987. Research and Development Series, BSD Ltd., Wakefield.

Mansfield 1989. 'Competence and Standards', Bob Mansfield, in *Competency Based Education and Training*, ed. J.W. Burke, 1989, Falmer Press.

Mansfield and Mathews 1985. *Job Competence*, Bob Mansfield and David Mathews, 1985, Coombe Lodge FESC.

Mansfield, Mathews and Mitchell 1990. *Competence*, Bob Mansfield, David Mathews and Lindsay Mitchell, 1990, Falmer Press.

Mathews 1990. 'Evaluating Occupational Standards', David Mathews, in *Competence and Assessment*, No. 10. Employment Department, March 1990.

Mitchell 1989. 'The Definition of Standards and Their Assessment', Lindsay Mitchell, in *Competency Based Education and Training*, ed. J.W. Burke, 1989, Falmer Press.

Mitchell, Mansfield and Leigh 1989. 'Understanding Knowledge: the Final Report of the "Identifying and Accrediting Relevant Knowledge in the Building Society Section" Project', L. Mitchell, B. Mansfield, Alan Leigh, 1989, BSD Ltd., Wakefield.

NFMED 1989. 'MCI Guidelines – Certificate Level', National Forum for Management Education and Development, 1989, London.

NFMED 1990. *Occupational Standards for Managers*, NFMED, 1990, London.

Spencer 1983. *Soft Skill Competencies*, L. Spencer, 1983, Edinburgh SCRE.

Stanton 1989. 'Curriculum Implications', G. Stanton, in *Competency Based Education and Training*, ed. J.W. Burke, 1989, Falmer Press.

TA 1989. *Technical Advisory Group Note 2: Developing Standards by reference to functions*, Training Agency, 1989, Sheffield.

TC 1988. *Classifying the Components of Management Competences: A Report by the Occupational Standards Branch*, Training Commission, 1988, Sheffield.

Chapter 3 Management Learning Contracts

Answers

1. A learner and a trainer should also agree on an action plan, the resources needed, and how the learning will be measured.

2. The correct role of each of the parties to the contract is set out in the first section of this chapter. If they fail to play their role correctly:

- the learner/manager may be unwilling to learn, reluctant to risk setting targets for his/her learning, unwilling to take the initiative – wishing to be led or told what to do – and may give up when the going gets tough.
- the trainer may find it hard to listen, being more comfortable with a traditional instructing or lecturing style: he/she may fail to introduce the approach correctly and may become irritable and impatient when difficulties arise.
- the organisation may be so concerned with immediate pressures that no time or allowances are made for people who wish to develop, and there is no recognition of the achievements of those who complete MLCs.

3. Action Planning has less of an emphasis on assessment measures than the Management Learning Contract method, but otherwise is similar, being directed towards the development of competences.

Management by Objectives typically involves an agreement between a manager and his/her boss about what the manager will achieve before a certain deadline. There is an emphasis on assessment and on precise measures of achievement, but there is generally little emphasis on actual learning or development.

References

Boak and Stephenson 1987. 'Training Needs Analysis and Time Management', G. Boak and M. Stephenson, in *Industrial and Commercial Training*, Nov./Dec. 1987, 19(6).

Hall 1982. *In Opposition to Core Curriculum*, ed. James W. Hall and Barbara L. Kevles, 1982, Greenwood Press.

Hartley 1987. 'A committed future from a commanding past: the theoretical heritage for experiential learning', M.J. Hartley, 1987, Paper to the World Conference on Co-operative Education, Amsterdam.

Honey and Mumford 1982. *The Manual of Learning Styles*, Peter Honey and Alan Mumford, 1982, pub. Peter Honey.

Humble 1970. *Management by Objectives in Action*, ed. J.W. Humble, 1970, McGraw-Hill.

Keeton 1981. 'Converging theories of Experiential Learning', Morris T. Keeton, 1981, Paper to CEA, CAEL, NCSL, NSIEE sponsored conference, City University of New York.

Knowles 1975. *Self-Directed Learning*, Malcolm Knowles, 1975, Follett, Chicago.

Kolb 1976. *Learning Style Inventory*, David Kolb, 1976, McBer & Co, Boston.

NRMC 1987. The Contract Form, 1987, NRMC.

Pedler, Burgoyne and Boydell 1978. *A Manager's Guide to Self-Development*, by Mike Pedler, John Burgoyne and Tom Boydell, McGraw-Hill.

Revans 1980. *Action Learning*, R.W. Revans, 1980, Blond and Briggs.

Stephenson 1990. 'Competence, Self Development and Philosophy', Mac Stephenson, 1990, NRMC.

Chapter 4 Preparation

Answers

1. An explanation of the Learning Circle can be valuable to both Priming and Diagnosis in that:

- managers are more likely to accept the MLC approach, given this simple theory base.
- managers are more likely to tackle skill-development contracts.
- managers are better able to structure their proposal to identify what they want to learn – what particular skill, what aspect of knowledge.

2. Gaining the manager's confidence is a process of reassuring him/her about

- the method
- the potential
- the challenge
- the safety of disclosure
- the people

as described earlier in chapter.

3. The main drawbacks of self-analysis questionnaires are:

- they rely on accurate self-perception.
- they may limit self-analysis to certain categories (which may not be enough).
- they may have confusing links between questions and 'results' so that the manager feels very little ownership for what the questionnaire produces.

To overcome them you might:

- ensure the 'results' are only used as a starting point for self-analysis, not as a final answer.
- encourage or arrange for discussion of the 'results' with someone who can see the manager's development needs from another viewpoint.
- encourage or arrange other people to complete the questionnaire for the manager, to reveal other points of view.

References

AMA 1982. *The Generic Competency Model*, American Management Association, 1982.

Back 1982. *Assertiveness at Work*, Kate and Ken Back, 1982, McGraw-Hill.

Belbin 1981. *Management Teams: Why they succeed or fail*, R. Meredith Belbin, 1981, Heinemann.

Blake and Mouton 1985. *The Managerial Grid III*, R. Blake and J. Mouton, 1985, Gulf, London.

Boydell 1971. *A Guide to the Identification of Training Needs*, T.H. Boydell, 1971, BACIE.

Honey and Mumford 1982. *The Manual of Learning Styles*, Peter Honey and Alan Mumford, 1982, pub. Peter Honey.

Honey and Mumford 1989. *The Manual of Learning Opportunities*, Peter Honey and Alan Mumford, 1989, pub. Peter Honey.

Margerison 1979. *How to Assess Your Managerial Style*, C.J. Margerison, 1979, MCB, Bradford.

MSC 1. *Management Self-Development* 1981, Manpower Services Commission.

NFMED 1990. *Occupational Standards for Managers*, NFMED, 1990, London.

Noon 1985. *A Time,* James A. Noon, 1985, Van Nostrand.
NRMC 1988. *What is Management?* based on an original text by Neville Harris, 1990, NRMC, Washington.
Rowe 1988. *The Successful Self,* Dorothy Rowe, 1988, Fontana.
Woodcock and Francis. *50 Activities for Self Development,* Mike Woodcock and Dave Francis, 1975, Gower.

Chapter 5 Negotiation

Answers

1. Sometimes the manager will make unrealistic or vague proposals, where the contract is too large or the wording unclear. At this point, the trainer must intervene to produce a workable contract, but must do so in such a way the manager still feels a sense of ownership of the agreement.

2. Knowledge, Specific Skills, Generic Skills and Techniques.

3. The Project Approach concentrates too much on activity, on achieving short-term results, without a sufficient focus on how the results were achieved, what lessons this has for the future, how activities might be tackled differently in the future. In other words, it is about doing, not learning.

The cause of a number of Project Proposals from a group of managers is likely to be

- a very task-orientated company culture and/or
- inadequate Priming and Diagnosis and/or
- inadequate briefing of their bosses.

4. The model of an MLC to deal with a Performance Problem is:

- gather and record information on the problem: when it occurs, what are the symptoms, what are the possible causes.
- identify priorities in tackling the problem.
- identify techniques or best practices to handle priority areas.
- apply techniques over a period of time, and evaluate progress.
- specify an action plan for further development

References

AMA 1982. *The Generic Competency Model,* American Management Association, 1982.
Honey and Mumford 1982. *The Manual of Learning Styles,* Peter Honey and Alan Mumford, 1982, pub. Peter Honey.
NFMED 1990. *Occupational Standards for Managers,* NFMED, 1990, London.

Chapter 6 Assessment

Answers

1. Evidence depends on the opportunities available, and the suggestions here are by no means intended to be definitive.

(a) Coaching Skills: perhaps definition of what 'coaching skills' are; a detailed account of a specified number of coaching skills; a self-evaluation of strengths and weaknesses. An audiotape would be a helpful addition.

(b) Proactivity: an account of a specified number of occasions when the learner has been more proactive than previously; testimony of line manager or other suitable person to support this; statement evaluating own feelings when being proactive; assessment of barriers to proactivity and an action plan for the future.

(c) Assertiveness: understanding of the difference between assertive, aggressive and passive behaviours; understanding of the concept of assertiveness 'rights'; this to be demonstrated orally, in an interview. Personal report on a specified number of situations when it was difficult to be assertive, although the learner wished to be. Analysis of barriers (thoughts and feelings) and of desired behaviour. Action plan for handling a specified number of particular types of problem situation. The individual should also demonstrate assertive behaviour when he/she delivers this report to the trainer.

(d) Report Writing: specified number of examples of before and after reports; with a verbal analysis of the improvements. (Some specification of the type of reports, the influence of company style in layout and language, will be necessary.)

Explanation in each case of the purpose of the report (and possibly the validity of the stated objectives to be agreed by the line manager or another witness) and how the 'after' reports meet these objectives. Possibly an action plan for further improvement.

2. The criteria would be contained, partially, in the specification of evidence, particularly where a number of occasions, or a number of pieces of evidence are produced.

Otherwise, criteria may draw on:

- The credibility of the personal report: the learner who claims he has been very assertive but is unable to meet the trainer's eye when he makes this claim must be challenged.
- The accuracy or reasonableness of the individual's understanding. The assertiveness contract sketched above refers to fundamental ideas on which assertiveness is based. The learner should have a thorough and accurate knowledge of those ideas. The coaching contract is more

open-ended: there are number of different ideas about the skills necessary to be a good coach. The learner should be able to explain a plausible, reasonable framework.

- The degree of improvement: more proactivity and better reports are required for those contracts.
- The degree of achievement or of self-understanding: if the 'after' reports are still of appalling quality, or the coaching sessions are very poor, it may be that the contract should not be considered complete. Alternatively (depending on contract) the important issue may be one of whether the learner realises the poor quality of what he/she is doing and makes realistic plans to improve.

References

Powers 1987. 'Enhancing Managerial Competence: The American Management Association Competence Programme', Edward Powers, *Journal Management Development*, 1987, 6(4).

Chapter 7 The role of the trainer

Answers

1. Realistically some experience and familiarity with the Tutor role is necessary if you are going to be effective as a negotiator and assessor of MLCs. You might consider your strengths and needs areas, and those of any colleagues, in respect of the Tutor role if you are considering developing a negotiation and assessment capacity.

2. 'Talk me through this: what is involved?'
   'How long will it take to do this part of the contract?'
   'How much time is involved?'
   'What is the main objective: the thing you most want to do?'

3. 'What are you going to learn?'
   'This looks to me like a project: what actual learning is involved?'

4. 'This looks great, let me make sure I understand what you aim to do. Talk me through it: your first learning object is . . .'

5. 'How are we going to assess this objective, here?'
   'What do you suggest we do about this objective?'

References

Rackham and Carlisle 1978. 'The Effective Negotiator', Neil Rackham and John Carlisle, 1978, *Journal of European Industrial Training*.

Chapter 8 The training triangle

Answers

1. The contribution a line manager makes to an MLC depends on his/her own skills and attitudes.

(a) Computing skills: contribution may be: arranging access; allowing some release from normal working; suggesting a problem or a set of data which could be used; verifying the accuracy of the data produced on the computer.
(b) Financial analysis: contribution may be: providing guidance on appropriate techniques to learn; arranging access to suitable inform-ation; allowing some release from normal working; verifying the accuracy of the analysis or the realism of the information used.

2. Line managers may behave in unhelpful ways:

- if they are unsure of the role they should play.
- if they fall back on more usual behaviours when they relate to the learner/manager: being directive or protective.
- if they have few skills experience of developing others.
- if they are under pressure to produce short-term results.

3. Line managers may sometimes be motivated by:

- reminding them that they are stewards of the human resources of their organisation, responsible for longer-term development as well as short-term results.
- assuring them that what they are being asked to do is not dreadfully difficult, can be productive and enjoyable, and has been used elsewhere with good effects.

References

Singer 1979. *Effective Management Coaching*, Edwin Singer, IPM.

Chapter 9 Range and scope of MLCs

Answers

1. The concept of staged development is important to the MLC because it leads the manager to set realistic and more clearly defined targets (in the form of assessment measures) and encourages an analysis of the components of the competence.

2. When a learner/manager requests to learn counselling skills, the dangers are:

- misunderstanding: 'counselling' is taken to mean a wide range of things, from counselling staff over domestic problems to a type of disciplinary interviewing. The trainer should ask, 'What do you mean, counselling skills?' and try to get a picture of what the manager wants to be able to do.
- impression: defining staged improvement in this area is not simple.
- lack of opportunity: real development in skills only takes place through practise. There is a danger that an opportunity to practise will not be available, or that it will involve a risky dependency.

3. The learning objectives could target analytical skills and organisational skills, or the interpersonal skills needed to gain access to people and obtain information, or the skills of maintaining a positive presence and self-confidence when faced by opposition.

References

Belbin 1981. *Management Teams: Why they succeed or fail*, R. Meredith Belbin, 1981, Heinemann.

Boyatzis 1982. *The Competent Manager*, Richard E. Boyatzis, 1982, Wiley.

Harris 1969. *I'm OK You're OK*, Thomas A. Harris, 1969, Pan.

Honey & Mumford 1982. *The Manual of Learning Styles*, Peter Honey and Alan Mumford, 1982, Peter Honey.

NFMED 1990. *Occupational Standards for Managers*, NFMED 1990, London.

NRMC 1990. *What is Management?*, from an original text by Neville Harris. NRMC, 1990.

Thomas 1975. 'Conflict and Conflict Management', Kenneth Thomas, in *The Handbook of Industrial and Organisational Psychology*, ed. Marvin Dunnette, 1975, Rand McNally.

Chapter 10 Case studies: systems, stress and time

References

Back 1982. *Assertiveness at Work*, Kate and Ken Back, 1982, McGraw-Hill.
Harris 1969. *I'm OK You're OK*, Thomas Harris, 1976, Pan.

Chapter 11 Case studies: impact, interviews and motivation

References

Belbin 1981. *Management Teams: Why they succeed or fail*, R.M. Belbin, 1981, Heinemann.
Melrose Films. 'More than a Gut Feeling'.
NFMED 1990. *Occupational Standards for Managers*, NFMED, 1990, London.
NRMC 1990. (1) *What is Management?*, based on an original text by Neville Harris, NRMC, 1990. (2) *Managing People*, based on an original text by John Rosser, NRMC, 1990. (3) *Operations Management*, based on an original text by John Bothams. NRMC, 1990.

Chapter 12 The learning organisation

References

Peters and Waterman 1982. *In Search of Excellence*, Thomas J. Peters and Robert H. Waternman Jnr., 1982, Arthur & Rowe
Schon 1972. *Beyond the Stable State*, Donal Schon 1972, Ancogan Page

Index